BORN IN POST WAR BRISTOL

Born in Post War Bristol

From Bomb Sites to Test Flights

COLIN HOLCOMBE

Colin Holcombe

Front cover image:
St.Mary le Bone Church Tower:
 courtesy of Bristol City Archives Ref; 39864/2/469

ISBN: 978-1-3999-3192-2

Copyright © 2022 by Colin Holcombe

All rights reserved. No part of this book may be reproduced in any manner whatsoever without written permission except in the case of brief quotations embodied in critical articles and reviews.

First Printing, 2022

Acknowledements

Dedication

I should like to dedicate this book to those dear friends and family members who are no longer with us and whom I was privileged to know.

Acknowledements

I should like to thank my family, and all those who, either knowingly or unknowingly, have enriched my life and provided me with much of the material, and background for this book.

I should also like to acknowledge the staff at the Bristol City Records and Archives Office for the help and support they provided, during my research.

ISBN: 978-1-3999-3192-2

Contents

Foreward		1
1	Introduction	3
2	My story begins	27
3	Memories of Abertillery	81
4	Conversations about the War	99
5	Bristol City Centre as a Port	129
6	Chandos Rd and Senior school	141
7	Holidays	161
8	The Hall and Rohan Years	181
9	Self Employment	217
10	My Book Shelf	249
11	Cold War and the Bristol Bus Boycott	257
12	Bristol's Legacy	277
13	Oh! I Almost Forgot	301

Foreword

Bristol, like many cities in the UK, suffered dreadfully during the bombing raids of the Second World War - indeed, as Colin has pointed out, it was the fifth most heavily bombed British city. Following the fall of France, Bristol was suddenly within easy range of the enemy, and many areas were left mutilated by raids. The city's port and aircraft industry, for which it was famous, made it an obvious target, and because of austerity the post-war rebuild was painfully slow.

Growing up, like Colin, in the battered old city, it was easy for us kids to take our bombed surroundings for granted and play happily among the ruins. We had little thought then about how fortunate we were to be the first generation not required to fight for our freedoms as our parents and grandparents had been forced to do.

Nevertheless, looking back down the years, our own stories about post-war times must seem, to the current generation, to be from another planet. The general sweep of the time is well-documented by historians, but it is people like Colin who bring the period alive with their own recollections, coloured with personal experiences, while living through what was a tumultuous time.

As an exact contemporary of Colin's and a friend from school days, it was interesting for me to track his footsteps while I had been pursuing my own path. In the 80s I became a member of Bristol Savages (now 04 Arts), and I was pleased to read the section concerning the Club. We all share memories of many of the major events recounted by him, but someone else's perspective somehow makes it more real, and brings the time and place vividly to life again.

This is a book which is a valuable record of the post-war time, seen through the eyes of an observer who knows that it is the small details, recalled decades on, which brings the period to life. If you are of a certain vintage and have lived in or near Bristol, reading this book will probably make you say, as I did, "Oh yes, I remember that! I had forgotten...."

Steve Foulkes

Chapter 1

Introduction

It was a difficult decision for any twelve-year-old boy to make as both guns had their merits. The pepper-box revolver was in near-mint condition, not a scratch on it, and although there was no maker's mark, the London proof marks were clear as a bell and it was decorated with some fine quality etching. The only drawback was the £12.10s price tag. The other weapon, a small percussion pocket pistol with folding trigger, was only £10.00, well within the eleven pound budget that resided in my pocket. It too had London proof marks and no maker's name, but this gun also had a small section of the walnut stock missing.

I was only a young lad, and although I was well versed, even at that age, in the concept of "doing a deal", I lacked the confidence to open negotiations with an adult dealer, so I just kept examining the two pistols.

Quinney's antique shop in which we stood was located on Park Row, a road that runs between the bottom of St Michael's Hill in Bristol, to the top of Park Street and the Will's Memorial Building. It was owned by a dealer who specialised in antique weaponry, but whose first name I sadly forget. He was familiar with both my father and myself, as my father ran a successful second-hand furniture business and had dealings with all the antique trade in and around Bristol. It was also quite well known that his younger son, me, collected antique weapons.

The pepperbox revolverI purchased

The shop owner could clearly see my dilemma, and decided to open negotiations on my behalf. "You look as if you're unable to make up your mind as to which gun to buy, is that because of the price of the pepper-box?" he asked smiling.

"Well yes" I replied, "I only have eleven pounds with me, I'd prefer the pepperbox, but I havn't got enough money to pay for it".

"Well look," he said, "your dad and I are doing deals all the time, so why don't we do the same. I'll drop the price of the pepper-box to eleven, and we can shake on a deal, how does that sound?"

It sounded good to me! Not only was I now the owner of super looking pepper-box revolver, but I felt as if I had just participated in an extremely grown-up negotiation, and dad would be pleased. As we shook hands on the deal, Quinney added, "For future reference, although I'm sure your dad has already told you this, never pay the asking price, you can always get some discount if you ask."

The outcome of the encounter was that I walked out of the shop eleven pounds poorer, but with a brilliant new addition to my burgeoning collection tucked under my arm, wrapped in several layers of newspaper and a brown paper bag, I hasten to add. Well! You wouldn't expect him to just let a twelve-year-old walk out of his shop carrying a gun, even if it was a black powder weapon that was perfectly legal to own.

You may find what you have just read rather shocking, but as I am always trying to explain to my granddaughters, things were very different back then, and it all seemed normal to us at the time. L.P. Hartley said, "The past is a foreign country: they do things differently there," and he was right. It's not right to judge people or things that happened in the past by our ideas and standards now. All sorts of things that were regarded as acceptable then would be frowned on, or even illegal now. We no longer flog young offenders, and women have the same rights as men in law.

Health and Safety was beginning to make its mark as well I remember, although many of my playgrounds when I was growing up were only semi-cleared bomb sites, and I clearly remember that the only heating in our bathroom consisted of a one-bar electric fire.

Now I suppose if I am going to tell the story of what it was like to grow up in Bristol from 1948 until the latter part of the century, then I had better go back to the beginning. I'll start by introducing the main players, and the stage on which the larger part of my story has been acted out.

Bristol

Bristol Coat-of Arms

Located on the River Avon, the City and County of Bristol was once a major trading port and a starting point for journeys of adventure and discovery, among which was John Cabot's voyage to North America in 1497.

Bristol's reputation has been tarnished in recent years by the role its port played in the slave trade during the 18th century, and the fact that much of the city's wealth was derived from it. Recently the Victorian stature of Edward Colston was torn down and thrown into the the city docks.

By 1672, Colston had become a merchant in London. He traded in textiles from London while importing oils, wine and sherry from Spain and Portugal, as well as trading different commodities with Italy and Africa.

In 1680, Colston became a member of the Royal African Company, which had held the monopoly in England on trading along the west coast of Africa in gold, silver, ivory and slaves from 1662, and had been establised by King Charles 11. Colston was deputy governor of the company from 1689 to 1690. His association with the company ended in 1692.

During Colston's involvement with the Royal African Company from 1680 to 1692, it is estimated that the company transported over 84,000 African men, women and children to the Caribbean and the rest of the Americas, of whom as many as 19,000 may have died on the journey. The slaves were sold to labour on tobacco and sugar plantations.

In 1681 he probably began to take an active interest in the affairs of Bristol, after investing in a sugar refinery. In 1682, he made a loan of £1,800 to the Bristol Corporation, and the following year, he became a member of the Society of Merchant Venturers.

Although a Tory High Churchman and often in conflict with the Whig corporation of Bristol, Colston transferred a large segment of his original shareholding to William III at the beginning of 1689, securing the new regime's favour for the African Company. The value of Colston's shares increased and being without heirs he began to donate large sums of money to charities.

Colston used his money and power to promote order in the form of High Anglicanism in the Church of England and oppose Anglican Latitudinarians, Roman Catholics, and dissenter Protestants. He withdrew from the African Company in 1692, but continued working on his private businesses until he retired in 1708. Colston was then an MP for Bristol from 1710 to 1713.

Colston died on 11th October 1721, aged 84. His will stated that he wished to be buried simply without pomp, but this instruction was ignored. His body was carried to Bristol and was buried at All Saints' Church. His monument was designed by James Gibbs with an effigy carved by John Michael Rysbrack.

Colston supported and endowed schools, houses for the poor, almshouses, hospitals and Anglican churches in Bristol, London and elsewhere., which is why his name features widely on Bristol buildings and landmarks.

In 1691, on St Michael's Hill, Bristol, at a cost of £8,000, he founded Colstons Almshouses, and at a cost of £600, the merchant's almshouses in King Street. He also endowed Queen Elizabeth's Hospital school.

Colston Almshouses St Michael's Hill
Bristol City Archives

Edward Colston's statue
Bristol City Archive 40826/PLQ/9

In 1696, at a cost of £8,000, he endowed a foundation for clothing and teaching 40 boys, and six years afterwards he expended a further sum of £1,500 in rebuilding the schoolhouse. In 1708, at a cost of £41,200, he built and endowed his great foundation on Saint Augustine's Back, for the instruction, clothing, maintaining and apprenticing of 100 boys; and in time of scarcity, during this and next year, he transmitted some £20,000 to the London committee, to be managed by the Society of Merchant Venturers for its upkeep. He gave money to schools in Temple (one of which went on to become St Mary Redcliffe and Temple School) and other parts of Bristol, and to several churches and the cathedral.

The Colston Society, which had operated for 275 years commemorating Colston, latterly as a charity, decided to disband in 2020.

In 1895, 174 years after Colston's death, a statue designed by John Cassidy was erected in the centre of Bristol, to commemorate Colston's philanthropy. Colston's slave-trading activities were subsequently uncovered in a biography of his life and work written by H.J. Wilkins in 1920, and from the 1990s onwards, there were growing calls for the statue to be marked with a plaque stating that he was a slave trader, or taken down.

In July 2018, Bristol City Council, which was responsible for the statue, made a planning application to add a second plaque which would "add to the public knowledge about Colston" including his philanthropy and his involvement in slave trading, though the initial wording suggested came in for significant criticism from members of the public and a Bristol Conservative councillor, with the result being that the plaque was reworded. This wording was edited by a former curator at the Bristol Museum and Art Gallery, creating a third proposal which was backed by other members of the public, though it was criticised by the academic behind the first two versions, who claimed it "sanitised" history, minimising Colston's role, omitting the number of child slaves, and focussing on West Africans as the original enslavers. Nevertheless, a wording was subsequently agreed upon and the bronze plaque was cast. After the plaque was physically produced, its installation was vetoed in March 2019 by the Mayor of Bristol, Marvin Rees, who criticised the Society of Merchant Venturers for the rewording. A statement from the mayor's office called it "unacceptable", claimed that Rees had not been consulted, and promised to continue work on a second plaque.

On 7 June 2020, the statue was toppled and pushed into Bristol Harbour by demonstrators. The statue was retrieved from the harbour four days later by Bristol City Council, and taken to a secure location. After the statue was toppled, the Merchant Venturers said that it had been "inappropriate" for them to have become involved in the rewording of the plaque in 2018, and that the removal of the statue was "right for Bristol".

From 4 June 2021, the statue was put on display in its damaged condition by Bristol's M Shed museum.

The port has now moved from Bristol Harbour in the centre of the city, to Royal Portbury Dock, located on the Severn Estuary at Avonmouth, where it remains a major port.

As well as having a historic port, Bristol has also contributed a great deal to the Aviation industry, (one of my particular interests, alongside antique firearms), and was the birthplace of many famous aircraft, such as the Bristol Boxkite, Bristol Fighter, Bristol Bulldog, the Blenheim, the Beaufighter, the Britannia, the Brabazon, and of course, possibly the most beautiful aircraft ever built, Concorde, to name just a few.

Proudly boasting two universities and two football teams, it is also a centre for the arts, where many well-know names started their acting careers at the Bristol Old Vic Theatre School, and The Bristol Hippodrome which opened in 1912 and is now designated a grade ll listed building, and boasts one of the largest stages outside London

Great engineering triumphs, such as the Clifton Suspension Bridge, the SS Great Britain and the Great Western Railway, can also be laid claim to by Bristol, thanks to its association with Isambard Kingdom Brunel.

I could go on citing Bristol's famous people, buildings and great heritage here, but instead, I will attempt to do them justice as and when they crop up in my story throughout the book, although perhaps this is the right time to try and answer a question that confuses a lot of people, including Bristolians. "What County is Bristol in?"

Well, since 1373 Bristol has always been a county in its own right, with its formal and legally recognised title being the "City and County of Bristol" when two settlements of Bristol to the north of the River Avon, and the parishes of St. Thomas, Redcliffe and Temple to the south were united. The common confusion often arises due to the differences between what classifies a city, county, and the lesser-known unitary authority, and also because Avon is still offered as a choice on many forms and drop-down menus.

There has been a settlement on the site since the Stone Age, and there have been some Roman finds in Kingsdown, and on St. Michael's Hill, although nothing to equal the wonderful Roman findings in Bath (Aquae Sulis) nearby. In fact, there is little evidence to suggest a Roman or any other settlement of any size on the site, until a mint was established in the Saxon burgh of *Brycgstow* (bright dwelling). The change in the form of the name to "Bristol" is most probably due to the local pronunciation of "ow" as "ol".

After the Norman Conquest of England in 1066 a number of motte-and-bailey castles were ordered to be built, and it is likely that Bristol Castle was started at this time on the orders of Geoffrey de Montbray, who held Bristol at the time, and was one of the Knights who accompanied William the Conqueror to England. The town of Bristol rose to prominence during the Noman era, gaining a charter and county status in 1373, when Redcliffe and Bedminster were incorporated into the city

On the 1st April 1974, (Yes, some people still say it was all a joke,) the county of Avon came into existence, the County of Avon incorporated the county boroughs of Bristol and Bath, part of the administrative counties of both Gloucestershire and Somerset, as well as Thornbury, Weston-super-Mare and several other smaller administrative areas.

Many might still refer to Bristol as being part of Avon, but this is not the case. The county of Avon was formally scrapped on 1st April 1996 and was replaced with four smaller unitary authorities, including The City and County of Bristol, South Gloucestershire, North Somerset and Bath and North East Somerset. Despite these changes the name Avon stubbornly refuses to go away, and still exists in the names of many of the region's businesses and institutions, such as, Avon Fire and Rescue, and Avon and Somerset Police, to name just two.

Now that question has been answered, I will introduce the main players in the early part of my story.

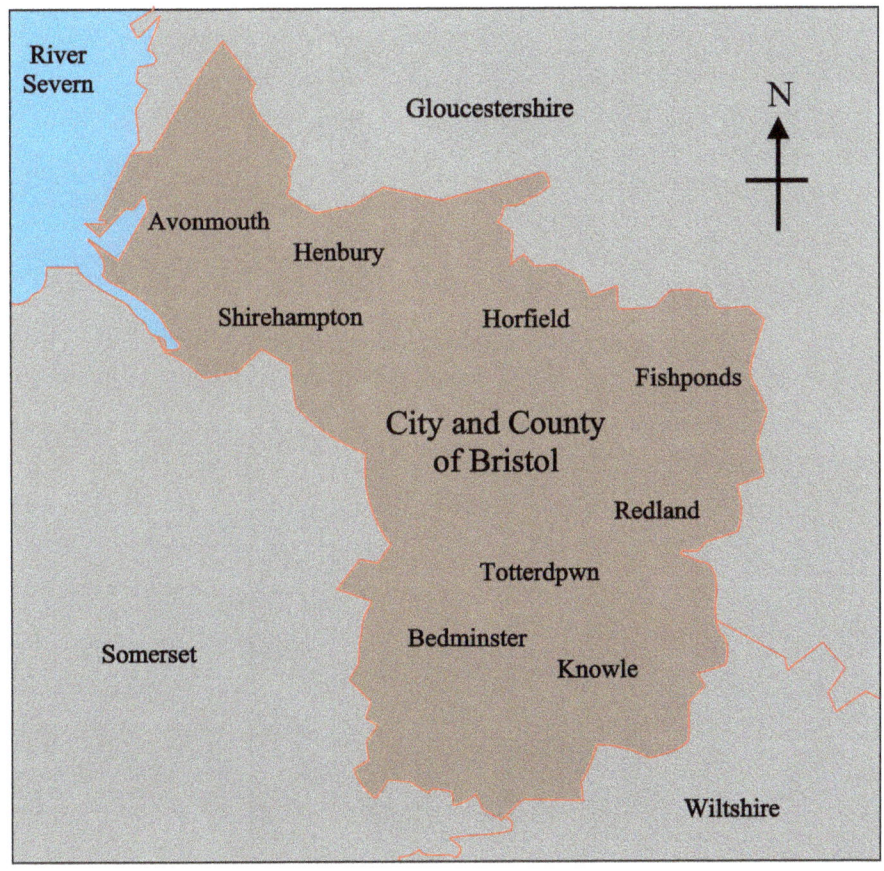

My Mother: Gladys Irene Langley.

Gladys Irene Lanley 1930

Mum had three sisters, Florence, Marjorie and Cissie and one brother, Jacob George. She moved to Bristol with her best friend Bertha, to work in service.

In fact, I later found out that it was Bertha who first introduced her to my father. At the time they first met, my father was driving a motorbike and sidecar, and would often take mum over the Aust ferry and on to Abertillery to visit her mum and dad there.

My parents married in 1939 at St Peter's Church on Castle Green. Sadly, the train from South Wales was delayed on the day and my mother's family arrived late and missed the service.

My father's parents were not pleased with his choice of bride, apparently wanting him to marry someone whom they had selected as a potential daughter-in-law. In fact, they boycotted the wedding altogether, causing a family rift that never healed.

It was only after my father died and I started to look into my family history, that I began to understand a little more of what had taken place.

My Father

My father was born in 1914, and had always been very reluctant to talk about his early life and family. He always signed himself R. F. P. Holcombe, the initials apparently standing for Ronald Frederick Phillip. However one day when he was chatting to my friend Phillip Pobjoy and myself, Phillip mentioned that his first name was really Roland, but because he didn't like the name Roland, he always used his middle name Phillip.

My father photographed in the back garden of 59 St Michael's Hill

My father then confided to us, uncharacteristically, and quite out of the blue that he also had the name Roland but didn't use it. This was a total surprise to me and for some reason that confidence, although never repeated, stuck with me.

After my father died in 1991, I decided to do some family research. Over the years I had learnt that there had been a falling out between my father and his parents, who lived in number 5, Woodbury Lane, off the top of Blackboy Hill.

They did not attend dad's marriage to my mother in 1939 at St Peter's Church on Castle Green, and my contact with them was limited to a quick visit on our way to Abertillery to celebrate Christmas with mum's parents.

On these occasions mum and dad would stay in the car outside 5, Woodbury Lane, while my brother and I were sent in to visit, and collect our presents.

I remember these visits as being quite strange, and that my "grandfather" was bedridden, and would be sat up in bed wearing a flannel nightshirt and night-cap like a character from a Dickens novel, and my grandmother would be sitting in a Windsor chair beside a large open fire and range.

The only picture I have of them, shows them standing outside number 5 Woodbury lane with my father in what I think might be his school outfit.

My father with his adopted parents outside 5 Woodbuy Lane c1920

All I knew for sure about my dad's childhood, was that he had attended St. Johns School, which was situated at the top of Blackboy Hill and where my brother also started his education.

I had been told that his dad worked as a haulier for the railways, and my father told me that he remembered an occasion when his dad took him to the stable and showed him the team of horses.

I therefore, had always assumed that he had started school at St John's when he was age five, but on researching the records of St John's, I discovered that he had in fact, only started there at seven years of age, and that his previous school was listed as Moorfields.

On looking through the records of Moorfields School at the Bristol Records Office, I could find no trace of a Ronald Holcombe, however, when I scrolled down to look for a birthday, I found that a Roland Frederick Phillips, with the same birth date, had been enrolled in the care of somebody called, Hatten.

I knew that when I was young, mum and dad were very friendly with a family called Hatten, so it was too much of a coincidence. Roland Frederick Phillips had to be my father, who had once said his first name was Roland, and signed himself with the initials R.F.P.

I later discovered that his real mother was Florence Phillips, and she had given birth to him in a workhouse in Fishponds, Bristol. I believe Florence was in the workhouse just for the birth, as she and her baby were discharged into the care of Florence's mother, one Annie Jones, (nee Phillips), at 19 Chapter Street, Dean Lane, Moorfield, Bristol. His birth certificate states "Father Unknown, religion, nonconformist."

Just how my father ended up being called Ronald and raised by Mr and Mrs Holcombe of 5 Woodbury Lane I shall never know for sure, but simply because of the timing, I speculate that his mother Florence probably died in the great influenza pandemic of 1918/19, in which over 50 million people died worldwide, and a quarter of the British population were affected. Young adults between 20 and 30 years old were particularly susceptible and the disease struck and progressed quickly in these cases.

It was nicknamed 'Spanish flu' simply because the first reported cases were in Spain, and as this was during World War One, newspapers were censored. Germany, the United States, Britain and France all had media blackouts on news that might lower morale, so although there were influenza cases elsewhere, it was the Spanish cases that hit the headlines, indeed, one of the first casualties of the strain was the King of Spain.

During the Second World War my father worked for BAC (Bristol Aeroplane Company) repairing aircraft at various airfields around the country.

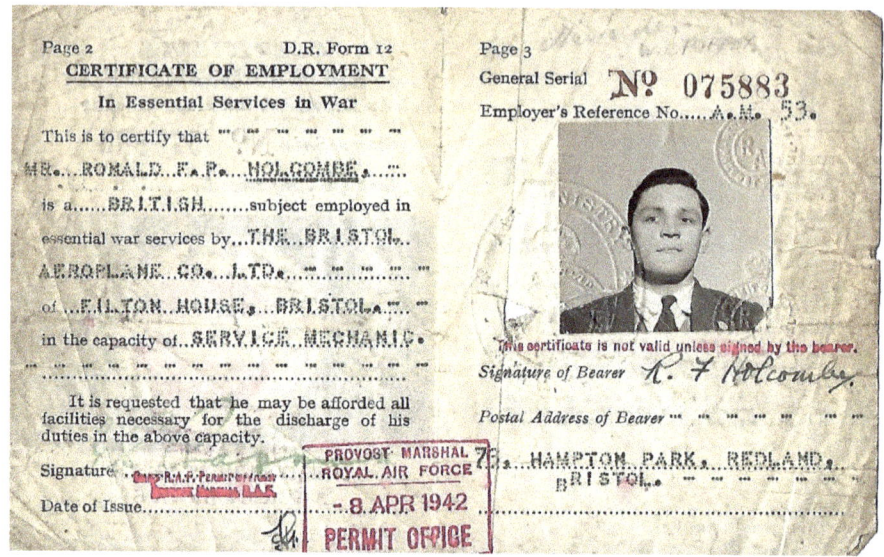

Dad's identity card during the war

He explained to me once, that when he went to enlist in the army, one of the questions he was asked was if he had any knowledge of "stress and strain". Well, my father had passed a City and Guilds exam on building construction during his training as a plumber, and that had covered the stress and strain in roof construction. "Right," said the recruitment officer, "it's aircraft maintenance for you," and packed him off to the BAC at Filton.

After the war he returned to the building trade, but always the entrepreneur, and propably with his new knowledge of air-frame construction, he also started to manufacture some caravans, trading out of number 1 Woodbury Lane, where he and my mother were living at the time.

The caravans themselves must have been constructed at his builders' yard in Hampton Lane, off Cotham Hill. I suspect he had a contact at a garage who made the caravan chassis for him.

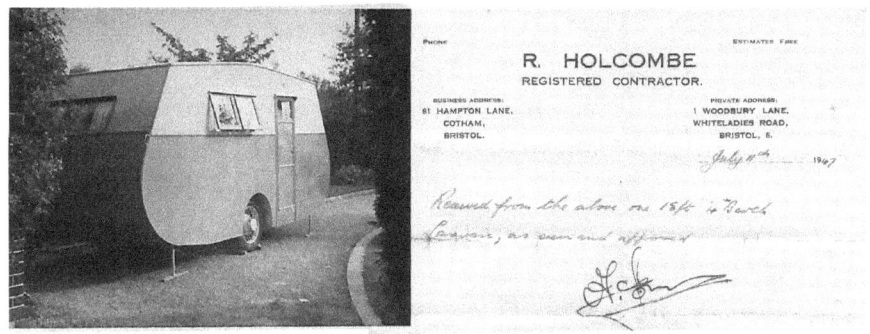

One of the caravans dad made and an invoice for it

My Brother Ronald

Brother Ron as my best man

I'm not sure when I first became aware of the fact that I had a brother, but because he was some seven years older than me, it wouldn't have meant a great deal anyway, the age gap between us was too great for us to attend the same school or play together, other than a crude form of cricket in the backyard of 59 St Michael's Hill with dad, even though we shared a bedroom up until we moved to Chandos Road when I was ten.

I think it's probably fair to say that Ron was the brainy one who passed his eleven plus exam and attended Cotham Grammar School, while I was the practical one who could solder a pipe by the age of nine, as well as wire a plug and make things out of wood, but failed the 11 plus exam and attended Bishop Road Secondary Modern.

Ron started work with the inland revenue when he left school. It seems funny now, but I can remember him leaving for work in a dark suit, a bowler hat and carrying a furled umbrella, as most Civil Servants did back then. Fed up with office work, he was persuaded by dad to go into the second-hand furniture business. When the bike shop opposite 6 Chandos Road came up for sale, our father helped him to buy it and they went into business together, running the two shops as R F Holcombe and Sons. Presumably the plural sons was either so I didn't feel left out, or he already had plans for me as well. The business wasn't generating enough profit for two, so Ron worked in sales for several years, finally choosing a career in insurance. He married Janet Sergeant, the elder of two sisters whose father ran the post office in Chandos Road. Ron and Janet have a son Andrew, so at least the family name has a male line and a chance of continuing.

John Newbury (My Cousin)

My cousin John Newbury

John Newbury was the only son of my aunt Flo from Abertillery, and was the only member of the family that I remember socialising with, both when I was younger and as an adult.

John was always the one to do things with me when our families got together. He would take me to the Bristol City Musem, the Zoo and Observatory, and if we were over in South Wales, we would often go to see a film at the local cinema or sometimes we would go to Crickhowell and either swim in the river, or just watch the anglers fly-fishing.

He was also the only member of my family I ever remember having a drink or playing darts in a pub with. Later when he met and married his wife Sue they would sometimes come over to stay for the weekend. John and I would visit a pub, or sometimes a casino and bring back a take-away for the four of us; they were good times for us, and when we both had young families we would still do things together, even sharing a self catering apartment on holiday in Rimini, Italy, or nearer to home in St Ives, Cornwall.

Me (Colin Holcombe)

Me in the back Garden of 59 St Michael's Hill c1955

Things were certainly changing in 1948. I came into the world on the 1st June, closely followed on the 5th July by the National Health Service. I'd never thought about it before, but as I was born some weeks before the NHS, my parents must have paid for the facilities and midwife.

The Second World War had only ended three years before, Mahatma Gandhi had been murdered earlier in the year and Israel had just become an independent state, despite the protests of the Arab states about the displacement of Arab Palestinians. Big mistakes were made with the best of intentions, and the consequences are still with us today.

1948 also saw the founding of The Democratic People's Republic of Korea, (North Korea) and the U.N. that had been founded in 1945, adopted the Universal Declaration of Human Rights, and formed the World Health Organization (WHO.)

As if all that wasn't enough, I'm reliably informed that while I was only recently home from the Bristol Maternity Hospital, and entirely blameless in all things, my older brother Ronald, named after our father, and my cousin John Newbury, who must have been over on a visit from Abertillery in South Wales, managed to take the handbrake off dad's car, which was described to me later as a large open tourer with running boards and exterior handbrake, and let it run a little way down Woodbury Lane, where we lived at the time.

I was actually born in the Bristol Maternity Hospital, originally known as the "Temporary Home for Young Girls Who Have Gone Astray," (or just "The Temporary Home). In 1865, it was located at number 9 Alfred Place, Kingsdown.

To start with, the medical facilities were secondary to providing a refuge for "unmarried girls" who had fallen pregnant. Young mothers would remain for three months after giving birth and were then found a position in domestic service, while their babies were placed "in the charge of respectable women." It was basically a form of forced adoption.

The Hospital then moved to number 50 Southwell Street, and was later known as the Temporary Home and Lying-In Hospital from 1894 until 1914. After the First World War, the hospital was used by an increasing number of married women such as my mother, and in response to this increased demand, Southwell House was extended and a home for the babies of unmarried mothers was established in cooperation with the Waifs and Strays Society. This is where I was born. On 5 July 1948 the Bristol Maternity Hospital was joined with the Royal Hospital, the Eye Hospital, the Children's Hospital and the Dental Hospital to form the, "United Bristol Hospital." In

1970 the maternity hospital moved to Queen Victoria House, near the Downs at the top of Redland Hill.

Southwell House with extention
Bristol City Archives. Ref; 43207/23/10/5

Bristol Materity Hospital Queen Victoria House

This is where our daughter Karen was born, and most Bristolians will remember it as being the large building opposite to the entrance of the The Glen, a popular night club. It was a favourite place for young people to meet in the late 1950s and 1960s.

Situated in a former quarry at the top of Black Boy Hill, the site included a dance hall with a milk and coffee bar in one building, and a social club, in another. Today it is the site of a purpose-built private hospital.

Former site of the Glen

The Bristol maternity unit then moved back to its roots in the new St Michael's Hospital on the corner of St Michael's Hill and Southwell Street, where our second daughter was born, on the site of the old 6th Battalion The Gloucesters.

The two following photographs show the same site at the top of the hill. The only remaining part of the original Head Quarter is the front wall that the railings were on. If you look at the house to the left, you can see that this is the house with the ivy covered wall in the original picture.

St Michael's Hospital on the site of the old 6th Glos HQ

The 6th Battalion, Gloucestershire Regiment HQ
Bristol City Archives: Ref: 43207/27/3/011. (The original image has been altered)

Chapter 2

My story begins

Pre-school

I can remember nothing of living in Woodbury Lane, but I understand that my grandparents lived in number 5, the last house on the left, and my parents lived further down the lane with my brother and the newly-arrived me in number 1.

The only things I know about my short time there came to light many years later, when it was reported that a famous person had left a baby behind, completely forgetting that they had a child with them. It turned out to be not such a rare occurance. Apparently in the late forties and early fifties when prams were much larger than now, mothers would often leave babies outside shops in their prams, whilst shopping. Evidently my own mother once returned home alone, after shopping, only realising when asked where I was, that she had left me in my pram outside Woolworths on Blackboy Hill! Thank goodness, it would seem that nobody else wanted me either, and I was still there when she returned.

I keep being reminded that attitudes were so much different back then, even if we were always told as children, "Never except sweets from a stranger!" nobody would think a baby in a pram was at risk in a busy main road.

Could that be me circled in red
wooliesbuildings.wordpress.com

My earliest actual memories are of living in a flat over a garage at number 39 Cotham Hill. Just when we moved there from Woodbury Lane I don't know exactly, other than it must have been before June 1953, because I remember the family's excitement when dad arrived home with a second-hand television, so that mum could watch the Queen's Coronation, the first time such an occasion had been televised.

On the ground floor was a garage that I can remember was called King's Cars, and was really just the basement of number 39. There was always at least one car for sale I remember, parked on the tiny forecourt, left of a steep flight of stone steps leading to the front door.

Actually, my earliest memory is of being anxious or uneasy as my mother negotiated her way down with me sitting in my pushchair in front. As my mother tilted the chair backwards so the rear wheels could roll over the front edge of each step, it felt as if I was strapped in a roller coaster going over the top, looking into empty space.

Our first television set was something like this one

Some years later, I was told that either Mr King himself or one of the men who worked for him, was in the habit of hanging his coat on the gas tap in the workshop, and that this resulted in the gas pipe fracturing one night, causing a gas leak. Luckily my family were awake and smelt the gas, meaning that no tragedy unfolded. Thank goodness my father was a plumber and knew what to do to turn off the gas. He later said that at one time, he was holding me in his arms out of an open window so I would breath fresh air and clear my lungs.

My father was running his own building firm at the time and rented a yard in Hampton Lane, at the back of our flat. An exciting place for a young boy. What I remember of it was that it had an open yard with racking for timber and scaffolding and a building at the end that was used as an office and store.

On one occasion Ron was helping our father get some wooden planks down from the shelving in the yard, and I must have been in the way, because I ended up having a cut just above my eye where the length of wood hit me. Even now the scar is just visible if you know where to look.

I think that my father was running that side of his business down at the time and moving into a new line of work as a furniture dealer and upholsterer, certainly not long after that time he ran such a business from a shop in Alma Vale Road.

39 Cotham Hill

My father employed an upholsterer to work in the shop, who everybody called "Pop" and I can remember him working at the back of the shop wearing a brown overall coat. If I was at the shop I would stand and watch him at work, stretching the seat webbing with a special tool and picking up the tacks with a magnetic hammer, the first time I had ever seen such a thing.

My father had trained originally as a plumber in the days when they were more than just pipe fitters and gas engineers. A large part of his work was on roofs, fitting the lead gullies and flashing, as well as fitting the gas and water pipes in houses.

A plumber's job was a varied one back then. Lots of houses still had gas lighting, and lead pipe was used for both gas and water. I can remember my father teaching me how to solder a lead pipe and "wipe" a joint when I was little more than ten. This involved expanding the end of one pipe with a dressing tool, to accept the end of another pipe that had been cleaned for soldering, priming and lighting a paraffin blow lamp, soldering the two pipes together with plumber's solder and flux, and then "wiping" the joint. This last bit consisted of applying extra solder around the joint and wiping it into a smooth shape, by heating it until pliable and wiping it with a piece of brown paper covered in candle wax.

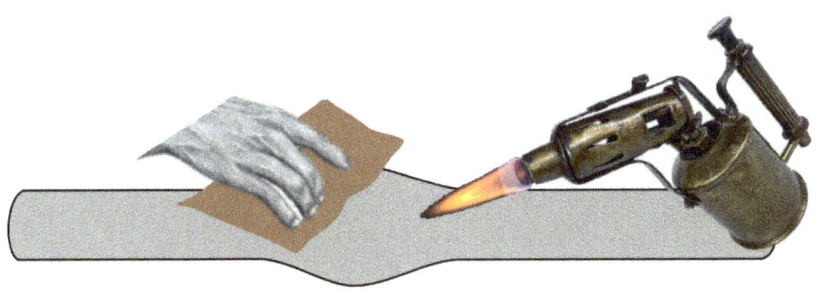

Wiping a lead joint

Up until I started work at fifteen, apart from woodwork and metal work classes at school, my father had been my tutor in all things practical. Thanks to him I could solder a pipe, change a ball-cock in a cistern or a washer for a tap; I could wire a light or power circuit in a house, paper a room, cut glass and upholster a drop-in chair seat.

Now I seem to be getting ahead of myself a little bit, so where was I, oh yes, 39 Cotham Hill. I can remember the layout of our flat in Cotham Hill, which was on the top floor. It had two large rooms at the front, one of which was our living room; the other was a bedroom that I shared with my brother Ron, and there were two rooms at the back, one was the kitchen that also served as a dining area. Back then all our meals were family sit down meals. The other back room was my parents bedroom, but if I ever saw the inside of it, I have no recollection of it. There was a toilet opposite the top of the stairs, but bath night would have been just once a week.

I've already mentioned that my brother Ron is seven years older than myself, so we had little in common growing up. That never really changed as we grew older, Ron was the brainy one who went to Cotham Grammar School, and I was the practical one who was good with his hands but couldn't spell for toffee and failed the eleven plus exam.

Now although he still had a builder's yard in Hampton Lane, I think our father must have started his second-hand business by then, because I remember there were some unusual items sharing the flat with us, one of which was a tiger-skin rug, with head still attached. Mum was for ever washing or polishing items that arrived wrapped in newspaper in a cardboard box, that when clean, were carefully re-wrapped and taken away again. This was something that happened right up until dad closed his last shop. There was always a drawer that contained not just the tins of Kiwi shoe polish, but the various cleaning products mum needed such as Brasso, Dura-glit and Vim scouring powder. We were taught early on to alway check that the contents of a bottle matched the label, and that tins could always be full of tacks, buttons, you name it   .

Cleaning products mum would have used. The bottle of Tizer, could well have been full of White Spirit!

It's likely that I will mention more than once that we used to spend the Christmas holiday in Abertillery, South Wales, with my mother's family, and there is one anecdote about it that I remember being told, from when I was very young.

Apparently, when I was still a baby, my father borrowed a car for a certain fateful Christmas journey, *(no, not that one)*, from one of his friends, a Mr. Edwards, who was the proprietor of a small men's outfitters at the junction of Cotham Hill and Hampton Lane.

Well, it appears that the roads were quite icy at the time and my father somehow managed to roll the car. No ABS brakes back then. Fortunately, we all escaped with no major injuries. I have never been told how Mr Edwards received the news of his car's fate, although I do know that he and dad remained friends, and I imagine the car was insured. I know they stayed friends, because when I started earning a living and buying my own clothes, I would often visit his shop.

Another memory I have from around that time was going into the Bristol General Hospital to have my tonsils removed. I remember being in a large ward with lots of other children. On the day I was to go home, I apparently had a slight temperature, and had to stay another night. I couldn't sleep that night because I was scared, being the only one in a vast empty ward after everyone else had gone home. Times are different now; they tend to discharge patients from hospital as long as they are still breathing and have somewhere to go. I still question my recollection of the occasion, wondering why all the children would have been discharged on the same day, but the memory of being alone is a vivid one. I even remember the kindness of the young nurse who came to check on me in the night when I couldn't get to sleep, and she sat on my bed reasuring me that mum and dad would be picking me up in the morning.

Bristol General Hospital has its origins in a small house in Guinea Street where it was established with 20 beds in 1832. Construction of a purpose-built hospital was started between 1852 and 1856 on land available because of the closure of Acraman's Ironworks.

The original building was designed by William Brace Gingell and an extension was opened by the then Duke of Edinburgh in 1891. Living accommodation for nurses, designed by Henry Crisp and Sir George Oatley, was completed in 1895 and extended in 1907.

1914 saw the addition of the King Edward VII Wing, a substantial additional clinical facility. In later years it became a rehabilitation hospital and after the building of the new South Bristol Community Hospital it closed in April 2012. The property was then acquired by a property developer who restored the ogee dome on the roof, that had been damaged by bombs during World War Two, and converted the building into apartments.

My own memories of the hospital, apart from having my tonsils out, was much later when my mother was transferred there from the Bristol Royal Infirmary, after breaking her arm in a fall. She was suffering with dementia by then, and had a care plan in place, so that she could still live at home on her own when discharged.

General Hospital now Luxury appartments

In the summer of 1953, we moved from the flat in Cotham Hill to number 59 St Michael's Hill, a house my father had purchased. Ever the practical man, he split the property into three flats, and we occupied the ground floor while the other two flats were rented out, to help pay off the £700. bank loan. One of the upstairs flats was rented out to a young couple. I can't remember their name, but I do remember mum pointing out that the husband was the spitting image of Bill Haley, of "Rock Around the Clock" fame, according to a picture of him she had seen in the morning paper.

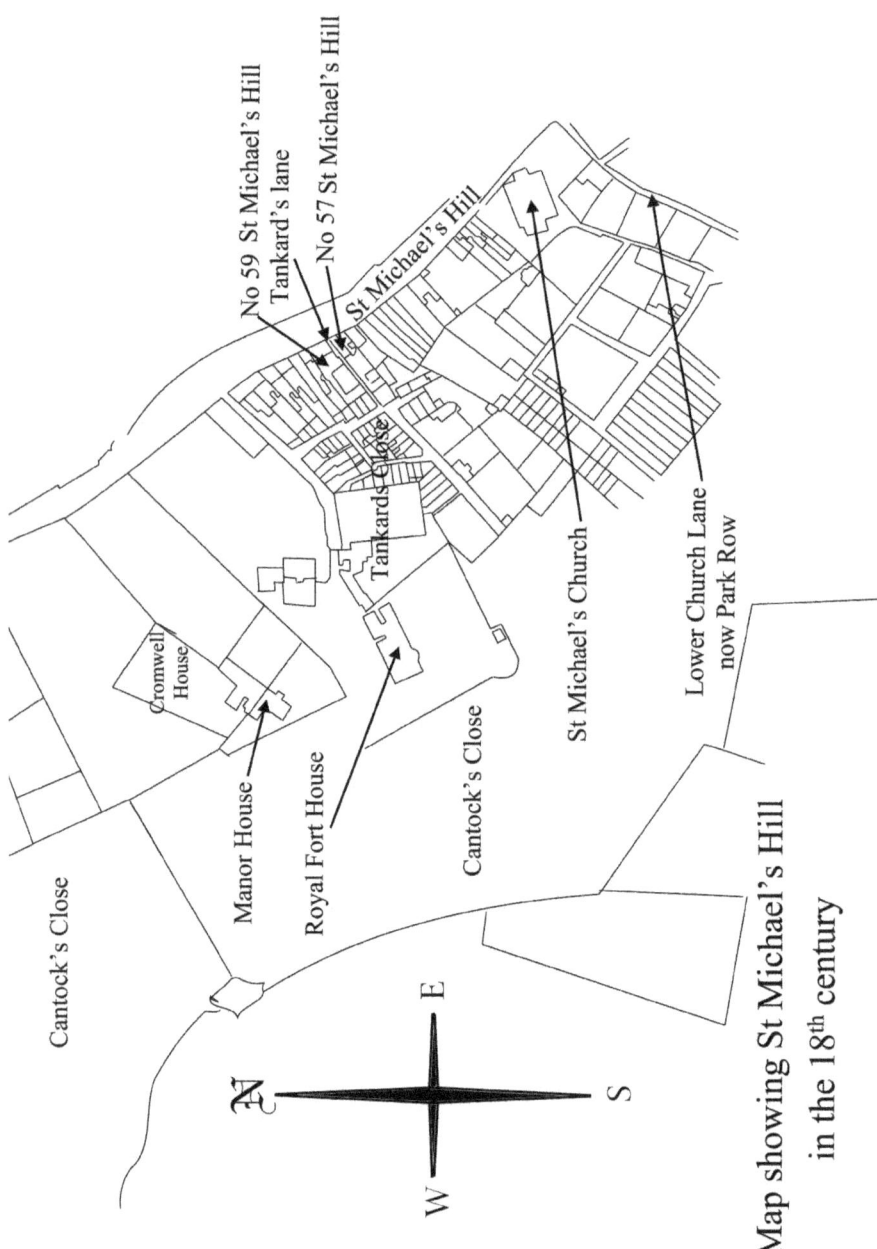

Map of St Michael's Hil

The house itself, one of first residences to be constructed on St Michael's Hill. was built sometime between 1709 and 1712 when it was occupied by Mr Francis Brickley, but the property seems to have quickly changed hands to a Mr Richard Ferryer. I have no idea how either of these gentlemen earned a living but they must have been quite well off to have afforded such a grand house.

Number 59 St Michael's Hill was a truly remarkable property, and made quite an impression on me over the few years we were there, even at a young age.

There was a large garden to both the front and back of the property, although the front garden was pretty much ignored as I remember, and looked much like it does in the following photograph. The back garden however, not only had a great tree for climbing, it also had sufficient room for my father to build himself a decent size workshop.

Apart from the three storeys you can see in the photograph shown below, and the large wine cellar beneath the property, there were two attic rooms with small casement windows that are just out of shot behind the parapet wall, due to the angle the picture was taken. The two rooms, were only ever used for storage, although they also came in useful for games of hide-and-seek with friends, which I was allowed to do, with the strict proviso that we made no noise upstairs to disturb the tenants.

As you ascended the first flight of stairs, you came to a small landing and a sharp left turn before ascending a few more steps to another half landing. From there you could either turn left again and ascend two more steps to the first floor, or go through the door facing you, that led through a kind of utility room that opened onto the garden at the far end. Windows on the left of this room looked out over the back yard. It was also the room in which some of us hid from a jumping jack one memorable bonfire night, of which more later.

59 St Michael's Hill: Inset: picture taken of me with my father outside the right front window

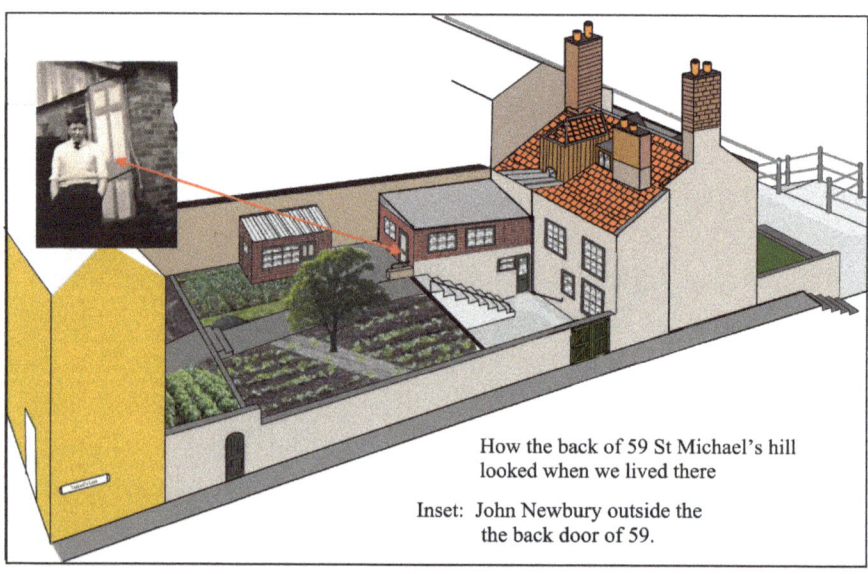

How the back of 59 St Michael's hill looked when we lived there

Inset: John Newbury outside the the back door of 59.

The back of 59 St Michael's Hill drawn from memory

The back garden was on the same level as the first floor and was accessed by way of stone steps rising from an enclosed yard at ground floor level, where we would draw wickets on a wall and play cricket. The yard itself was entered from the back door located in the kitchen, and had large double door that opened onto Tankard's Lane. Why such large doors onto such a narrow lane will remain one of the mysteries?

My brother and I still had to shared a bedroom, but as I was seven years younger, my bedtime was earlier than his.

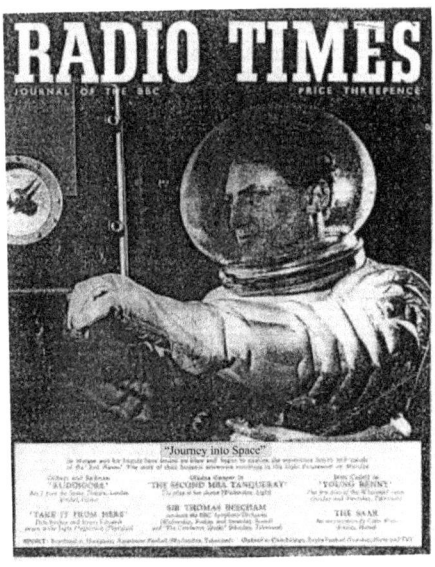

Radio Times 1954

However I had the privilege of being allowed to stay up late once a week, so that I could listen to "Journey into Space" on the radio with my brother. Journey into Space was the last scheduled radio program to attract a larger audience than the television.

When we first moved in, there was a lot of work to be done converting the property into flats and plumbing in a toilet and bathroom on each floor, although I think it's possible the tenants had to share a bathroom.

There were no skips in those days, and in any case, getting rubbish from the front of the house down to a vehicle parked on the hill outside would have been difficult, and would have taken a great deal of time and effort. My ever-resourceful father however, found a quick and easy alternative.

There had never been any intention of utilising the cellar, other than using the top few steps down to it as cool storage for milk and butter, (not many people owned a fridge back then), so my father made a large hole in the kitchen floor, and all the rubbish ended up being thrown down into the cellar, never to be seen again.

I was never allowed into the cellar, but I was told that there were stone wine racks there, and that rain water from the roof was ducted down into the cellar and ran in channels between the racks to cool the wine.

At that time I suffered from frequent and quite bad nosebleeds, and my parents would often have to get up in the night to administer help in the form of a cold compress. This was at a time when, although the first thing my father did was provide the property with a solid fuel boiler to provide hot water, we didn't have central heating for some reason

Perhaps my father considered the large bulky radiators of the time just too big for a domestic home, or it could have been to do with the positioning of tanks, and the fact that the property was split into flats. Whatever the reason was, my father decided that instead of venturing out into a cold passageway to access my room, he would put in a communicating door between the two bedrooms.

He marked the position and outline for the door in both rooms and began knocking through, knowing that the material under the layer of plaster would probably be stone. In this assumption he was correct. However what did surprise him was the thickness of the wall. It was so thick in fact, that when the job was complete, we had, not a communicating door, but a communicating passageway with a door either end. The wall turned out to have been almost two metres thick! We could never understand why an interior house wall should be built so thick, and nobody has ever come up with a plausible explanation.

However, one of father's customers at the time was, Elliott O'Donnell, a local ghost hunter and Bristol historian. He had always maintained that there was some treasure hidden somewhere between the two churches on St Michael's Hill, the Church of St Saviour with St Mary at the top, and St Michael's on the Mount at the bottom. He also said that such a thick wall could conceal a lot of secrets and suggested that it was probably part of a previous building on the site and that dad should investigate further, even taking down the rest of the wall.

A suggestion my father ignored. Maybe bacause I can remember him telling me one day, years later in fact, that he considered Elliot O' Donnell to be a bit of an odd chap, as he would pay money to sleep in houses that were said to be haunted. It was for that reason he was never taken seriously, at least by my father. However I discovered quite by accident recently, the following article on line:

"In 2012 students from Bristol University, found a secret door hidden in the side of a well-shaft, while searching for buried treasure under guidance of the spirit of a dead Nun, which is said to haunt a 17th, Century house on the lower slopes of St. Michael s Hill, Bristol. The four Bristol University Students dug until brickwork stopped operations. They were directed by Mr. Elliott O Donnell, the ghost hunter and psychic author. After two table-rapping seances at Midnight, in the house, which was built on the side of a Mediaval convent, Mr. O Donnell was led to an old well which has lain undiscovered beneath the cellers for perhaps more than four centuries. After digging for a further five feet, the students struck solid brick, which appears to be a brick wall, but which has a hollow ring and it is belived to conceal the entrance to a secret passage described at the seance".

Inset: Elliott O' Donnell directing university students searching for treasure

Impression of the communicating doorway My father made between bedrooms

Could the inset picture have been taken directly below the passage my father created?

I have tried to research the article further to discover if the house mentioned was number 59, but have come up against my own brick wall. I am however convinced that it was number 59, simply because it is one of earliest properties built on the lower slopes, that have been demolished, and which were in the ownership of Bristol University. I am also impressed by the simmilarity between the space shown in the inset photograph and the passageway my father ended up with. Is it possible the one is directly above the other?

I now find it distressing to think that, simply because numbers 59, 57 and 55, were going to block some light from the new university building that was due to be built, they had to be demolished. My father received a compulsory purchase order and was forced to sell.

The university had promised to develop the site, possibly with a small garden, but nothing was ever done. If you look at the site now, you would be forgiven for thinking it was a bomb site.

However, if it had been a bomb site it would have been redeveloped by now, if not with a building, then maybe a memorial garden with a sculpture to commemorate those who died in the Bristol Blitz.

Maybe the university will do something if the trees and bushes that have taken over the site, start to block the light from their building?

Looks like a bomb site but the Luftwaffe played no part in this one
Bristol City Archives Ref:452112/OF/4/46

I suppose in the end, you could say that my father being force to sell and look for another property, was the making of the family business, as combining his business and home properties under one roof proved to be a great success. That part of my story comes later.

The lane that ran up the side of the property separating number 59 from 57 was Tankards Lane, which provided access into Tankard's Close. Tankard's Close was first called, "Broome Hay" and later "Tinkers Close" on early maps, and must have had its name changed early on for some reason, possibly due to a change of ownership.

The right-hand side of Tankard's Lane going towards Tankard's Close was the boundary of our property, and there were doors opening onto it from our back yard. Further up the lane was a door that appeared to go nowhere, being under the end of our garden but beneath it. It seems odd to me now that my father never investigated it further.

Much of Tankard's Close was destroyed by bombing during the air raids on Bristol during WW11, and made an interesting playground for me and some of my friends on our way home from the boy's junior school that was just on the edge of the Close. However Tankard's Close was just one of many such sites around Bristol when I was growing up, but it was the most exciting. One of the bombed houses had the remains of the staircase, and with a carefully placed table and a leg-up we could reach it and climb to the first floor.

On the following map and photograph I have highlighted the positions of number 59 St Michael's Hill, together with my junior school and the buildings in Tankard's Close that were demolished in the war. The properties highlighted in yellow are the ones on the right of the next picture. The second picture shows the house where we could reach the first floor.

Tankard's Close just as I remember it. The houses on the right are highlighted in yellow on the following map.
Image courtesy of University of Bristol Library, Special Collections

House in Tankard's Close with remains of staircase we could reach
Image courtesy of University of Bristol Library, Special Collections

Map showing Tankard's Close as I knew it. The houses highlited in yellow are the ones shown far right in the photograph

Legacies of the Second World War were everywhere to be seen in the city in the fifties, or not to be seen as was the case with missing railings. The public were told that their iron railings would help with the shortages, and both private and council railings were cut down for the war effort. The most obvious legacies however, took the form of vacant bomb-sites, unrepaired houses, temporary prefabs and vacant sites that had been turned into allotments under the "Dig for Victory" campaign during the war.

The Dig for Victory campaign encouraged anyone with a garden to grow their own food rather than use valuable resources in transporting food from elsewhere.

Car ownership increased after the war and some of the larger bomb sites were tarmacked over and used as car parks in the city. The following pictures clearly illustrate the Bristol I remember when growing up. The one of the corner Bridge Street especially, although this particular photograph looks like it was taken towards the end of the 1960, judging by the cars in the car park. The prefabs shown in the last picture are typical of the ones I was familiar with, as a teenager growing up.

I can certainly remember there being gaps in ranks of shops all over the place like the ones in Park Street and knew it was because of the blitz, but I never stopped to imagine what actually would have been like at the time!

Corner of Bridge street looking towards St Nicholas Church

Bridge Street 1944 with St Nicolas Church on the left
Bristol City Archives 41969/1/7

Vacant lots in Penn Street

How I remember Park Street in the Fifties with the missing shops

My parents would have remembered it more like this
Bristol City Archives 41969/1/33

Examples of the type of Prefab I became familier with

School Days

My life as a shoolboy started in 1953, at St Michael's Church School at the bottom of St Michael's Hill when I was five.

The school building was located just behind the church, the full name of which was, "St Michael's on the Mount Without", the "without" part of it's name meaning that it was just outside the city wall. The original church on the site was Norman, the tower being added in the 15th century. Bells were installed in the tower in 1739, and by the 1760s the population of the city and parish had grown considerably and the church needed to be extended. One of my enduring memories of living on St Michael's Hill was the sound of the church bells on a Sunday morning ringing the changes.

A survey was carried out by Thomas Paty, an architect and mason who worked mainly in Bristol, and he described the fabric of the old building as "ruinous", and as a result, demolition of everything except the tower was undertaken and it was rebuilt.

The church finally closed in 1999 due to falling attendances and was boarded up. In October 2016 the building caught fire, and there were reports that the fire may have been started deliberately.

St Michaels Church after the fire

Eileen will remember the night of the fire especially because she was visiting Karen, our elder daughter, who was having radiotherapy as an in-patient at the BRI oncology department at the time, a very traumatic and worrying period for all the family. As Eileen left the car park, she recalls the sky seemed a strange colour, and she couldn't turn left towards the bottom of St Michael's Hill as she usually did, because the road was blocked off by the police. She admitted to me later that she got a bit lost trying to find a new route home; it was a stressful time for us all. In October 2017 the building was put up for sale and was bought in 2019 by local businessman, Norman Routledge, to restore as a performing arts venue.

My time in the Infant School was relatively uneventful and I made several friends there. It is one of the world's great mysteries that when comparing notes, when Eileen and I first started dating, we discovered that we had been in the same class at Infant School.

St Michael's Infant School Class of 54

The strange thing is Eileen had a photograph of the same class as shown above. Most if not all the same pupils and the class teacher are in her picture, except me, and there is no sign of Eileen in my picture shown here!

We have tried to locate Eileen's copy, which we can only assume was misplaced after her mum died and the flat was cleared out. The only explanation for the two different class photographs that we can think of is that for some reason they were taken on consecutive days, and that one day Eileen was off sick and the other I was having my short-wave treatment. Other than that I'm at a loss to explain it!

As I've just mentioned, it was during my time at St Michael's that I had to go to the Children's Hospital at the top of St Michael's Hill to have a course of "Short Wave Treatment".

This happened once a week for a while after my tonsillectomy at the General Hospital, and involved me sitting in front of machine, and having two round pads positioned each side of my head. The nurse would then set a timer and I would have to sit still for what seemed an eternity, but was probably fifteen minutes or so, with a buzzing sound coming from the pads.

The machine's timer was on the front of the machine where I could see it, and one day the nurse was called out of the room on some errand or other.

Medical shortwave treatment machine

She told me to sit still and that she would be back very soon. I was becoming anxious after a while, because I could see that the time was almost up, but there was still no sign of the nurse. I began to wonder what I should do if she wasn't back in time to turn it off, and was frozen to the spot when the time ran out and the alarm rang.

Fortunately for my sanity the nurse appeared only seconds after the timer rang, but the incident was traumatic enough to a five-year-old for me to remember it as if it was yesterday.

Childrens Hospital at the top of St Michael's Hill

One of the other places I remember from my time at St Michael's was further up the hill on the corner of Southwell Street, where the new St Michael's Hospital is sited now. In the 50s it was just an open area of land that was referred to as the Sixth Gloucester's. I only found out years later that it was the site of The 6th Battalion of the Gloucestershire Regiment HQ.

I think after the HQ closed, it must have had a drill hall and or firing range next to it at some time, because we used to get through the fencing that surrounded it and often found spent cartridge cases.

When I and my classmates started in the Juniors, the girls remained at the same building behind the church, but the boys moved up to the boy's junior school in Tankard's Close. My journey to and from the school was a short walk out of the double doors from our back yard into Tankard's Lane. across the remains of Tankard's Close and I was there.

Rear view of my junior boys shool in Tankard's Close
Image courtesy of University of Bristol Library, Special Collections

After a while the bomb site became a dumping ground for piles of what looked to me like twisted rusty steel bars. I didn't know it then of course, but these were the reinforcing bars to go in the poured concrete pillars of the new university building, that was to signal the distruction of our beautiful old house, as well as the school.

One event that stands out in my memory, and convinced me that corporal punishment should play no part in school discipline, was having the cane from Mr Long, in 1955 or 56. Mr Long is the one on the right of the four teachers in the photograph. I'm the boy fifth from the right in the same row, one away from him, and the impressive looking building you can see in the background, by the way, is the Royal Fort.

Pupils and staff of St Michael's Junior School, taken in the school playground

Mr Long had left the classroom for some reason and selected a boy from my class to stand at the front of the room and report to him on his return if anyone had misbehaved in his absence.

Class photograph taken in the playground, but this time with the Royal Fort behind the photographer

I think the boy next to me must have asked me a question and I answered him. When Mr. Long returned, he was informed that I had been talking in class, and both I and the other boy were called to the front to receive the cane.

Now corporal punishment was a new experience for me and I had no idea what sort of level of pain to expect as I bent over and touched my toes as instructed. Well, it would seem likely that because I was to receive only the one stroke of the cane, Mr Long had decided to make it count. The cane he used was a thin flexible rattan cane that he kept hanging on one of the coathooks attached to the outside of a storage cupboard in plain sight of the class.

I was determined not to cry in front of my classmates, but as I walked rather gingerly back to my desk after receiving my punishment, it felt as if I had just sat on a marine distress flare, the pain was excruciating, I was in agony. Although the pain eased as the day went on, it nevertheless remained with me for the rest of the day, and when I got home, it was immediately obvious to my parents that something was wrong.

I explained that I had received the cane for talking in class, and my father was concerned that I was still in pain after so long, and examined the site of my punishment. I have no idea what he saw, but he was clearly furious at the severity of the beating I had endured, and went to the school to complain first thing the next morning.

The following day, when Mr Long once again had to leave the room, I was made to stand in a corner facing the wall. Mr Long meanwhile, explained to the class that it was a precaution, in case I told my parents that I had the cane for nothing again, and that day I was teased by a couple of the other boys, suggesting that I'd been crying to mum and saying that I had been caned for nothing.

My father I remember, once again rather angry, visited the school again to put the record straight the next day, and although I never had the cane again, I did receive slaps with a ruler across the palm of my hand on numerous occasions, for what seemed the flimsiest of mistakes, even once, just for getting some sums wrong. This injustice I kept to myself however, whistle blowing just seemed to make things worse.

My time in Junior School greatly improved however after I left Mr Long's class, and fortunately I never had any dealing with the man again.

In the meantime Tankards Close slowly aquired its ever growing pile of twisted steel bars. The school building was demolished with the rest of Tankard's Close to make way for the new building., and to the delight of all of us, we were provided with two brand new purpose built classrooms adjacent to the Church Hall, and facing the old Girls Shool.

New junior boys classrooms built after Tankard's Close building demolished

I think the fact that the building was new and clean, and we were the first pupils to be educated there made us all feel a little more important. especially as we all had brand-new desks as well, and it was no longer an act of desperation to visit the toilets, as the new ones were nice and clean. It was also the first time I had ever been inside a brand new building. I can't describe how I felt, other than to say it was a new and strange environment to find myself in, like going on a passenger plane for the first time.

My best friend in junior school was Phillip Pobjoy, who lived with his adopted parents in Tyndall Avenue. Tyndall Avenue was a turning near the brow of the hill to the left, and the houses were semi-detached three-story buildings with an attic floor and first floor veranda that must have been built around the turn of the century.

These beautiful houses have all now gone, the same way as 59 St Michael's Hill, and been pulled down to make way for the university, an institution that seemed to be acquiring a great number of the historical buildings in Bristol, and was intent on destroying them, much like the city planners, and completing the job that Hitler's Luftwaffe had started.

I keep asking myself why, with so many bombsites and vacant plots like Tankard's Colse available close to the city centre, it was deemed necessary to pull down buildings that had survived the Blitz.

At the opposite end of Tyndall Avenue to St Michael's Hill, on the right-hand corner, and almost opposite the Hawthorns Hotel, was the University Botanical Gardens. These gardens were entered via a small gate that was never locked, so I can only assume that all were welcome.

Houses similer to the ones I remember in Tyndall Avenue, sadly now replaced with ugly concrete and glass office blocks.

My school friends and I spent many a happy hour playing within its precincts, collecting frogs and newts in jam jars and generally having a good time. It was one of our favourite playgrounds. I seem to remember a fossilised tree-trunk, but perhaps my memory is playing tricks now.

I do remember coming home with with a jar full of tadpoles so I could watch them turn into frogs, and wondering why some had disappeard while the others were getting fat. It was a few days before dad pointed out that I should have been feeding them, Ugh!

It was also around this time that I started swimming. We must have started going with the school, certainly I remember my class being marched up St Michael's Hil in twos, with my swimming trunks rolled up in a towel under one arm. We were taken to Kingsdown Swimming Baths, and Phillip and I would sometimes go on our own at the weekend.

Old site of the University Botanical Gardens with the original wall

Our other favourite places to play included the city docks, Brandon Hill's Cabot's Tower, Bristol Downs with the observatory and views of Avon Gorge and the Suspension Bridge, and of course, Bristol Zoo Gardens.

The Bristol Downs is an area of public limestone downland, consisting of Durdhan Down to the north-east, that is owned by the Bristol City Council, and Clifton Down to the south-west, separated by Stoke Road and owned by The Society of Merchant Venturers. (See Map on page 61)

Kingsdown Swimming Baths had one of the largest pools in Bristol at the time

Since an Act of Parliament in 1861, when Bristol Corporation acquired Durdham Down, the Downs have been managed as a single unit by the Downs Committee, a joint committee comprising members of both the Council and the Merchant Venturers.

The Guild of Merchants was founded in Bristol in the 13th century, and swiftly became active in civic life. It funded John Cabot's voyage of discovery to Newfoundland in 1497.

A replica of Cabot's ship The Matthew was built in Bristol in the mid-nineteen nineties and is now a huge visitor attraction in the city, alongside Brunel's SS Great Britain.

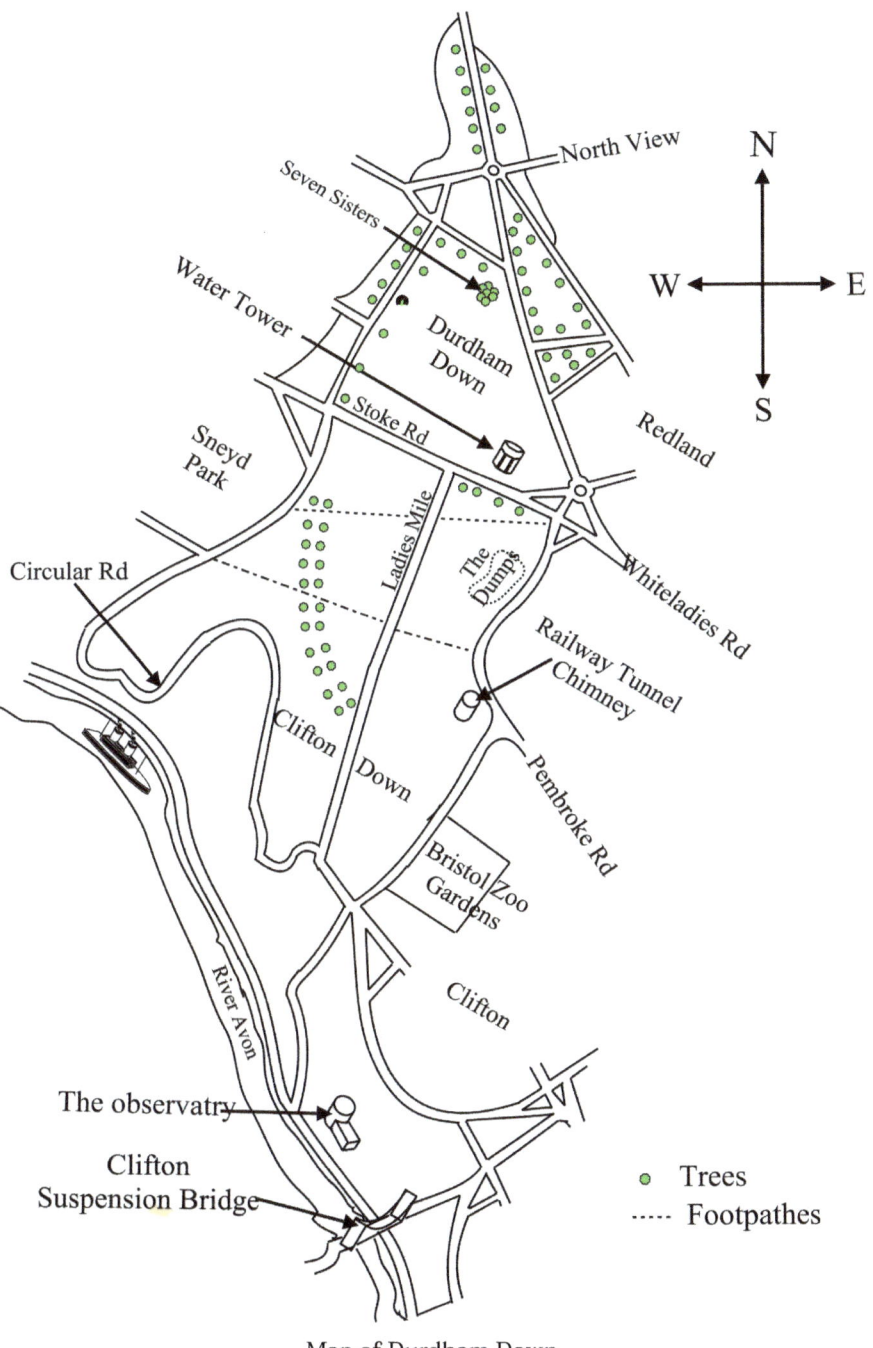

Map of Durdham Down

The society in its current form was established in 1552 by a Royal Charter granting it a monopoly on Bristol's sea trade.

During the eighteenth century many of the Society's members, including Michael Becher, John Duckenfield, Isaac Hobhouse and Edward Colston were directly involved in the slave trade, but one must remember that not all the members were in favour of the trade.

The society continued to contribute a great deal to the city and the welfare and education of Bristolians. It helped with the funding of the Clifton Suspension Bridge and the establishment of The Great Western Railway as well as many schools and colleges.

Replica of Cabot' ship The Matthew

However, despite all the positive things the society achieved and the charitable work it still does, the involvement in the slave trade by some of the Society's members, has sadly tarnished its otherwise positive reputation.

But I digress yet again, so getting back to my childhood playgrounds and the Bristol Downs, there were several areas where Phillip Pobjoy and I liked to spend our time. Among them the Dumps, the Sea Walls, the Observatory Camera Obscuar, and the stone slide and Brunel's Suspension Bridge to name a few.

The Dumps, or Tumps, are an extensive area of deep trenches that may date back to the seventeenth century, and are possibly the remains of old lead mines. This area was also quarried for calamine and limestone (for building and burning for lime). It's unclear why they were not levelled when the old quarries were filled in in the 1870s.

The deep areas have now largely been overgrown by scrub over the past fifty years and the area looks nothing like I remember it when we played there. Just down from the Dumps is what looks like a medieval tower, but is actually a chimney to clear smoke from the railway tunnel that runs under the Severn into South Wales.

Railway tunnel chimney

The Observatory, overlooking the Suspension Bridge and Avon Gorge was erected, with the permission of the Society of Merchant Venturers, as a windmill for corn in 1766 and later converted to grind snuff, when it became known as "The Snuff Mill". This was damaged by fire in 1777, when the sails were left turning during a gale and caused the wooden machinery to overheat and catch fire. It was in 1828 that William West, a Bristol artist, rented the building and installed a camera obscura.

The Observatory

West also built a tunnel from the Observatory to St Vincent's Cave, which opens onto St. Vincent's Rocks on the cliff face, 250 feet (76 m) above the floor of the Avon Gorge and 90 feet (27 m) below the cliff top.

Descent to St Vincent's Cave

Most visits to the Downs would involve a trek up to the observatory. However, I only once descended to the viewing platform in the face of the cliff, and although not afraid of heights, I found the slippery descent through the rocks to be an experience I disliked intensely.

We would however, always be facinated by the images the camera obscura projected onto the round white viewing surface and as we walked around the table, one of us would be holding the handle above our heads that turned the lens and focused the image in and out, altering the view.

The viewing platform

Camera Obscura Image table

It felt strange to see couples walking past the observatory or families picnicing on the grass, tottaly unaware that we were watching them.

These days I find that I can't often walk very far, not even a par five hole on the golf course, so I marvel at just how far we used to walk as kids. I would leave home on St Michael's Hill to call for Phillip, and we would then walk up the hill to the Homeopathic Hospital. We could then walk down Cotham Hill, and either turn left along Queens Road, or cross over to Clifton Down Station or continue up Whiteladies Road and Blackboy Hill to Durdham Down.

We would spend the day on the Downs or at the zoo, and then return home; our only instruction was to be home before it got dark.

Sometimes back then with Philip Pobjoy and later on with Alan Pegler, I would climb down the Avon Gorge, not so much on the rockface, but down the steeply sloping woodland, although there were on or two occasions when we did have to climb a small way on the rocks, much to the horror of anyone who spotted us from below.

Climbing down the Avon Gorge from the Downs to the Portway

The Entrance to Bristol Zoo Gardens

I honestly can't remember if we paid to get into the zoo, or even if unaccompanied children were allowed in under a certain age, but although we frequented the grounds often, we were never challenged.

Lion enclosure in the 1950s

Back then I never gave any thought to whether the animals were happy or not. I know now of course that some of the behaviour I witnessed, such as the big cats constantly pacing up and down, are signs that the animal was stressed from being confined in too small a space. Thankfully zoos are aware of this and are now adapting, and catering for the animals mental as well as physical needs, ensuring that they have the benefit of a nutritious diet a and vet on call if unwell.

Some argue that keeping animals in captivity is cruel, but most animals in the wild spend their lives hungry and face the horrible prospect of either being eaten by predators, or starving to death if unable to catch their prey because of even a minor injury.

The Monkey Temple

Two of our favourite sites were the Monkey Temple, and the penquins and they all appeared happy, but I have to admit that even as a youngster I did wonder if the brown bear had enough room in his bear-pit.

Bristol Zoo itself was founded on 22nd July 1835, by Henry Riley, a local physician. He led the formation of the Bristol, Clifton and West of England Zoological Society, in order to study the habits, form and structure of the animal kingdom, as well as affording national amusement and recreation to the visitors of the neighbourhood. One famous shareholder was Isambard Kingdom Brunel.

The bear pit.

The children's TV show "Animal Magic" was presented by Johnny Morris, who would combine jovial voiceovers applied to various animals with some basic educational features. It was filmed at Bristol Zoo, and probably the two most well known animals were Alfred the Gorilla, who's bust can still be seen at Bristol Museum and Rosie the elephant who would give rides to visitors, and who was walked by her keeper once a year down Blackboy Hill to be weighed on the weighbridge in the entrance to Cox and Sons builders yard at the junction of Whiteladies Road and Cotham Hill.

I can remember my father telling me this when buying plumbing fitting there. A lorry had stopped on the bridge to be weighed. I was suprised to see that it was basically a large balance scale. Instead of the lorry, I imagined the keeper holding Rosie still on the plate, while the man inside moved the weights along the balance arm in the same way that the school nurse weighed us.

If we weren't to be found at the zoo, the university botanical gardens or the Downs, the chances were that we had gone to Brandon Hill, the site of Cabot's Tower.

Family picnicing on Brandon Hill with Cabot Tower in the background
Bristol City Archives Ref: 40826/CAB/1

Brandon Hill was an amazing adventure ground that we frequented often between the ages of 8 and 11, although there was no playground as such. I do remember that there were some swings, it was ideal for hide and seek. It was cheap to go through a turn-stile and climb the steps to the top of the tower itself. Once at the top you an incredible view over the city.

Of course not all our time was spent away from home when playing. After all, number 59 had a large garden as well as easy access to Tankard's Close and Royal Fort Road.

View over the city from Cabot's Tower

One rather scary incident that happened while living on St Michael's Hill, came about because my father helped me to make what we referred to as a "dandy", but most people seem to call a soap-box racer.

Drawing of the "dandy" my father and I built

There were several streets that had enough slope for a decent run, but my favourite was Royal Fort Road. It was a good length to build up speed, and because it only led to the Royal Fort and a bombed-out Tankard's Close, it was seldom used by cars.

My friend Phillip and I would often have races, starting at the top of Royal Fort Road and ending at a white chalk line that we would draw across the road near to its exit onto St Michael's Hill. There were sometimes disputes about which of us had actually crossed the line first, so we once tried to rig up a finishing tape using a ball of wool. As luck would have it, this was one of the rare occasions a car decided to enter the road, and the driver was not best pleased!

One day, my dandy seemed to be in overdrive and I was well ahead of Phillip, but as I approached the finish line, the primitive hand brake snapped and I continued my journey out onto the hill. Luckily there were no cars coming down at the time. However, as I turned right heading down St Michael's Hill rather than continue straight into the wall facing me, it soon became apparent that stopping would entail almost as much risk as not stopping. A decision had to be made quickly as I was now increasing speed at a rate of knots. I didn't fancy crashing at the speed I was doing, so I tried simply putting my feet down to act as brakes. This resulted in my top half being tipped forward and the back wheels catching up with my ankles. Exactly what happened after that I can't remember, but the end result left me lying in the road with cut knees and a bump on the head. Nevertheless, some valuable lessons learned, the dandy was repaired and used again.

Memories of Bombfire Night

My father had always been one of those people who loved a good bonfire. I'm not saying he was a pyromaniac or anything even close, but I have to admit it seemed to be his favourite way to dispose of rubbish, and as a family we always enjoyed bonfire night, especially when we lived on St Michael's Hill. The large back garden meant that we could build quite a large one.

On one eventful 5th of November some family friends, Mr and Mrs Hatton and their son and daughter had been invited to join us for our firework party in the back garden. Mr Hatton brought with him a box of mixed fireworks, which he placed on the ground a sensible distance from the magnificent fire my father had built. Nevertheless it would seem that a spark from the fire did manage to reach the box, and all hell was let loose.

My mother, brother, Mrs Hatton and I hid in the utility room behind the back door that was on the same level as the garden, closely followed by a jumping-jack, and my father was last seen escaping down the stairs to the back yard, closely followed by Mr Hatton and a rocket.

A Jumping-Jack

Jumping Jacks, were small fireworks which you would light and which then burned in an erratic way, jumping all around the garden with sparks and crackles. The UK government decided at some point in the late nineties that Jumping Jacks, along with some other fireworks such as bangers and mini-rockets, were simply too dangerous in terms of erratic flight and banned them from sale to UK consumers.

Fortunately, even though the dangerous situation gave everybody a nasty scare, nobody was hurt and it remains a bonfire party never to be forgotten.

Memories of going to auctions.

I can always remember being taken on calls with my father to buy furniture from peoples houses, and I would often be left in the car or van outside while dad went in to do the deal. He would always tell me he wouldn't be long, but after a while I would begin to get anxious. When I got a bit older, he would take me in with him, and I soon picked up one or two tricks of the trade on how to close a deal.

Sometimes, during the summer holidays, I would spend the day at an auction with my father, and I got to know a few of the dealers he was friendly with. I remember that Lalonde Bros & Parham's auction rooms were located somewhere near Lloyds Bank on Queens Road near the Triangle. The frontage onto Queens Road was no more than a door leading into a large room at the end of a long corridor. I remember that on the right-hand side there were vertical racks where items such as doors, divan beds and mattresses could be stood on end.

My father would sometimes purchase a mattress, if it contained horsehair, as this could be put through a machine that would clean and fluff it up ready to be reused in upholstering furniture. Horsehair was an expensive alternative to flock, and used only for the best quality furniture or restoration.

If there were mattresses for sale, we would squeeze them to see which were filled with flock and which were horsehair. Sometimes, unscrupulous dealers would take a pocketful of flock with them to the auction, and if they found a horsehair mattress, they would make a small tear in it and insert some flock, and leave it protruding so that anyone else looking would assume it was stuffed with flock and not bid on it. I'm sure my father, however, was far too honest a dealer to resort to such unscrupulous actions, and it must have been some other dealers I saw doing it.

It was a fairly common practice for dealers to put items into auction to dispose of them if they had been in stock for a long time, in order to cut their losses and clear space for fresh stock. However, if other dealers recognised the item as belonging to a fellow trader, they would refrain from bidding on them, and the items would seldom realise their true worth. For that reason, many of the dealers, my father included, would enter items into an out-of-town auction rather than a local one, in the hope that they wouldn't be recognised.

I remember dad coming home furious one day because not only had a particular dealer recognised several items in an auction that belonged to my father, he had gone to the effort of writing the name *Holcombe*, in chalk on every piece, ensuring that none of the dealers present would bid on them. I think my father lost a lot of money that day.

Sometime later however he came home very happy with a van-full of new stock. He had bought several items at auction very cheaply that day, as none of the other dealers seemed interested in bidding on them. Asked over dinner that evening why he thought he had been so lucky, he confided that it could have had something to do with the fact that he had taken a piece of chalk with him that day, and written his name on all the items he was interested in. "The other dealers just didn't bid for some reason," he said with a smile.

In later years when I was running my own restoration business, I would love going to the auctions myself. Some of the furniture in the auction would of course be in need of repair or restoration, and if I got them at the right price, I would restore them and offer them to the trade in pristine condition.

Sometimes I would go with my friend Doug, (more of him later), and we would buy a piece together, to restore and sell in his shop on Gloucester Road. I remember being at Taviners auction rooms with Doug one day. It was situated in Prewett Street behind St. Mary Redcliffe Church, and was a favourite of ours because there was pub next door that served good pub food.

The site of Taveners Auction Rooms and the pub we frequented when attending.

On one particular day, there was a rather nice gateleg table for sale, but the joints were quite loose, so much so that one of the barley twist legs was completely detached. It had been wrongly catalogued as a nineteen thirties oak gateleg table, but I recognised that under the horrible thick varnish, it was in fact a Victorian walnut table, worth far more than a 1930s one. Doug was still concerned that other dealers would also recognise its true heritage, so to ensure we got the table cheap, he discreetly picked up the detached leg and slid it down his trouser leg.

"What the hell are you doing?" I asked, a little surprised by his action.

"Going for some lunch" he replied, walking out rather stiff legged.

After a moment's hesitation, deciding what I should do, and I confess, waiting to see if his dubious actions had been spotted, I followed him out. After lunch in the pub next door we were both a little nervous about bidding on the table, one leg of which had been relocated to the boot of Doug's car, but when we returned we managed to get it for a fair price. In the end we made a decent profit, but decided that we weren't cut out for that sort thing, it was far too stressful.

One item that I kept my eye out for when viewing an auction was a dressing table that could easily be converted into a writing desk. Dressing tables were out of fashion but desks were popular and fetched a good price. Customers often wanted a writing desk to go in a home office, or just somewhere for the children to do their homework on, rather than the dining table.

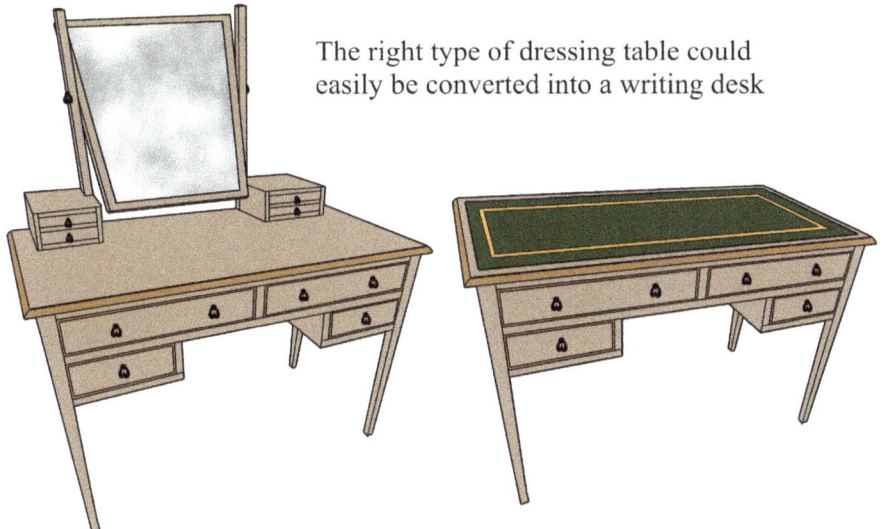

The right type of dressing table could easily be converted into a writing desk

Some dressing tables would make excellent writing desks

It's a fact that most of the items purchased at auctions are purchased by dealers, and in those days it was only the seller that was charged, usually 15 to 17.5% of the hammer price. The idea of charging a buyer's premium of 10% didn't start until much later.

It was the fact the dealers were bidding against each other that gave rise to the controversial, "Auction Ring." It was possible for a dealer to make a day's money at auction, even if he didn't actually end up buying any new stock.

The way it worked was this: dealers would view the auction as normal, making a note of the lot numbers they were interested in and the price they were willing to bid up to for it

Then they would get together before the start of the sale to compare notes. If several dealers were interested in, let's say, Lot 50 a mahogany bookcase, they agreed beforehand who would bid on it when it came up, and the other dealers would not bid against him, meaning that the selected dealer would be able to purchase the lot at a lower price, as there would be less bidding against him. This would happen on all the agreed lots.

After the auction was over the dealers would meet up at the local and auction the lots off again amongst themselves as follows: Let's suppose that the bookcase, that would normally realise a hammer price of £100, sold for £60, because of the lack of bidders. The item would be auctioned off again at a local pub. Whoever bid the most, let's say £100, would put the money in a kitty, and the dealer who purchased it at the true auction would take out the £60 he paid, leaving £40 in the kitty. When all the lots had been sold in this way, the dealer who purchased the lots they wanted, had paid the price they would have done anyway, but there was now a sum of money in the kitty that could be divided equally amongst the dealers in the ring. The practice was outlawed, and auctioneers were always on the lookout for it being in operation.

To be fair, auctioneers also had one or two tricks up their sleeves as well, and would sometime take a fictitious bid off the back wall, if they thought a dealer was about to win a lot that he would normally pay more for, forcing an extra bid. I've also suspected that if an item didn't look as if it was going to reach its full worth, and would maybe do better in a specialist sale, that the auction house would bring the hammer down, purchasing the item themselves, to sell later in a more specialist sale.

Chapter 3

Memories of Abertillery

    I have already mentioned that each Christmas we would travel to Abertillery in South Wales to spend the festive holiday with my mum's parents. They still lived in the same house my mother and all her siblings were born in, 16 Tillery Street. My mum's brother Uncle Jake was also still living there, and at Christmas when we descended, my cousin Sylvia would also join us for the Christmas holidays and sometimes bring a friend to stay. Just where everybody slept I don't know, except that when I was old enough to sleep in a proper bed, I shared the front bedroom with my brother Ron and my cousin John.

    There are memories, some good and some not-so-good that just stick in your mind for no obvious reason, and one or two of mine are from our Yuletide visits to Abertillery. Firstly, the fact that we always put decorations up, Chinese lanterns, and paper chains as well as holly and mistletoe. We had to be careful with the flammable paper decorations, because before I helped my father install electricity in 16 Tillery Street, it had only gas lighting. I remember being lifted up by either my dad or uncle Jake, box of matches in hand, so that I could light the gas mantle.

Outside 16 Tillery Sreet

I also remember being intrigued one year by the sight of large cooking pot in the middle of the dining table. I'm not sure how old I was, but I remember climbing up so that I could reach it and lifting the lid to investigate.

If I close my eyes, I can still see the contents even now, a sheep's head! Sheep's head stew tonight then....lovely.

One thing my mother taught me for which I am grateful, concerns money and gambling. It was a kind of tradition at Christmas for the family to all sit around the table in the front room and play cards. The game we played was called "Shoot," and there was no skill involved, it was pure gambling. Everyone woud collect small change in the days leading up to Christmas, knowing that it would be needed. The family would each take a turn at being the banker, which meant putting a sum of money in small change into a kitty in the centre of the table. The cards would be shuffled, and the bank would deal three cards to each player. The player would then have to bet on the likelihood of beating the top card on the deck, with a card of the same suit, and put some money in the kitty. The banker would then turn over the top card. If the bankers card won, then the money stayed in the kitty. However if the banker's card lost, you would take out double the bet you put in. If for instance, you had three high cards of different suits, you would have a good chance, and if you wanted, and had enough money, you could call "Shoot." meaning that you would match however much was in the kitty. If you won, the whole amount was yours and the bank would move on to the next player.

I was still quite young, but as it was Christmas I was allowed to stay up late, and go to bed at the same time as Ron and John. Of course, I wanted to join in and play, so my mother said that was fine, and gave me some change to play with. However, she explained that the money she gave me was mine to do with what I wanted. If I wanted to go to the toyshop and spend it that was OK, and if I wanted to play cards with it that was OK as well, it was my choice. The one thing she was adamant about however, was that if I lost the money playing cards, that was it! I would not be given any more to replace it. Of course, I lost, and it didn't matter how much I cried, the money was lost. I think it took a few days to sink in, but since then, even though I love a gamble, I have learnt never to gamble with anything I wasn't prepared to lose.

The route we took on our journey to "Abber" as we called it, was dependent on whether or not the Aust Ferry was working that day. If it was, then it made the journey by road much quicker and more exciting, as the alternative was a huge detour up to Gloucester, and then back down through the Forest of Dean, where we would break the journey with a picnic lunch, often eaten in the car if it was raining.

Joining the car ferry at Aust. This photograph looks to have been taken at a very low tide.

I can remember on one occasion the forest floor was a solid carpet of bluebells, and we ate in the car because mum thought they would stain our clothes or the blanket if we sat outside.

What I most remember best however was the Aust ferry and being in the car as dad drove onto the boat. The ramp just didn't feel safe to me as the man on the boat signalled to my father which way he should steer.

Picnic in the Forest of Dean and my first driving lesson in a Bedford Dormobile

I'm not sure what year we last used the car ferry at Aust; all I know is that the only times my parents visited "Abber" after the Severn Bridge was available, was after mum's parents and Uncle Jake had all died, and I drove them over to see Abertillery and the old house. I believe that was also my parents first experience of being on a motorway.

Soon the bridge would be finished and the car ferry would be redundent

My mother's other two siblings, my aunt Ciss and aunt Marge, both wed and moved to London, although I am not sure of the timeline.

Marge's married name was Kidney, and she, like Flo, had one son called John. I only met my aunt Marge and John Kidney on a couple of occasions, but when I was still at junior school, Aunty Ciss and Uncle Jack (Sylvia's parents), would often visit on their scooter and stay over.

I was alway pleased to hear they were coming because I knew they would always take me out somewhere as a treat. I remember visits to the cinema, if there was a film they thought I would like, or the seaside and sometimes the zoo.

The picture below shows us on the pier at Weston-super-Mare. Mum and dad must have driven on that occasion and taken this with the little box camera we had. It looks as if we had just visited the lifeboat station and had our pins. I remember there was a plastic model of the boathouse for donations. If you put coins in the slot at the top, the door would open and a little model lifeboat would slide down the ramp.

Weston-s-Mare with Aunty Ciss and Uncle Jack

One occasion that stands out for me was when Ciss and Jack took me into town, and bought me a 3-D viewer. It must have been quite expensive, and I can remember being told off after they had left for allowing them to buy such an expensive gift when it wasn't even my birthday. The item in question was a View-Master, and you could purchase a variety of different discs for it.

Sadly, Uncle Jack was involved in an accident when the scooter he was riding was struck by a car emerging from a sideroad, and spent the rest of his life unable to walk without crutches, and the visits sadly stopped

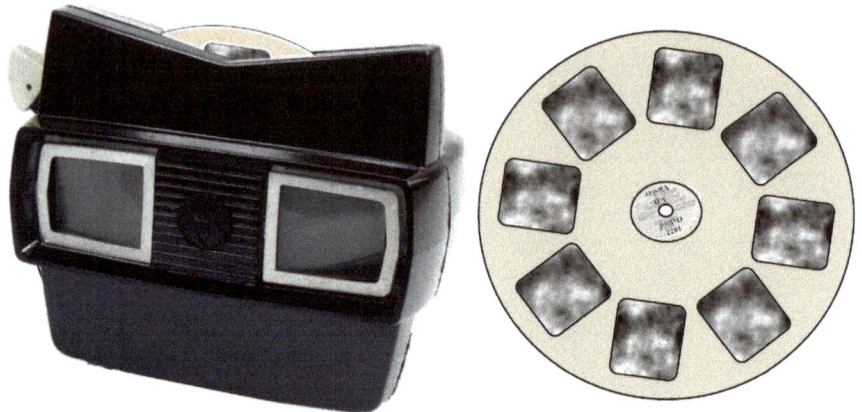

Image of the controversial View-Master

Aunty Flo apparently married and became Florence Newbury. However the marriage didn't last long after my cousin John was born, and she moved back to Tillery Street, before meeting the man who would become John's dad in all but name, Jack Brain (my other uncle Jack).

Flo and Jack Brain, with son John Newbury, were also frequent visitors to Bristol, and I think John must have been as familiar with the layout of Bristol Zoo and the Downs as I was, and he became more like a brother to me than a cousin.

Mum's brother, Uncle Jake, lived in number 16 Tillery Street all his life. I believe the only time he spent away was during the Second World War, when he was in the Welsh Guards and was part of the British Expeditionary Force that was evacuated from Dunkirk.

After being rescued from the beaches and landed back in Britain, he had to make his own way home, and apparently turned up at my parents flat in Hampton Park, looking very dishevelled and minus most of his equipment.

After surviving the war, he returned to Abertillery and resumed his work as a coal-miner at Six Bells Colliery.

On the 28th June 1960 he was waiting to start his shift, when there was an underground explosion which killed 45 of the 48 miners working in that part of the mine. It is now the site of the artistically acclaimed Guardian memorial designed by Sebastian Boyesen which commemorates the disaster.

The memorial, although primarily commissioned to commemorate those who died at Six Bells disaster, is now dedicated to all mining communities wherever they may be.

I was told, (but have no way of knowing the truth or otherwise of the statement) that the men who survived uninjured still had to finish their shift before being allowed home.

There were two cinemas we frequented as I remember, one in Abertillery itself and one in Brynmawr at the heads of the valleys. I seem to remember that the one in Brynmawr was rather smelly. I later discovered that when the building was converted into a permanent cinema in 1911, the front rows of seats were designed to be removed every Friday night, when trestle tables were laid out for the Saturday produce and livestock market, after which the wooden floor was disinfected. Nevertheless, the smell of the animals and discarded produce, as well as that of the disinfectant, would linger through the afternoon matinee film.

I also have a memory of seeing goats being led down Tillery Street and people coming out of the houses to purchase milk straight from the goat. Whether this was a regular occurrence or not, I can't be sure. I may even have dreamed it, but it was the first time I remember seeing a farm animal being milked.

Six Bells Colliery

I've already mentioned the fact that there was no electricity until my father installed it, and when we stayed, I would have to share a bedroom with both my brother and my cousin John. I can remember going upstairs to bed with a candle in one hand and a chamber pot in the other; it was all very Victorian. I had witnessed John extinguishing the candle by pinching the wick with his fingers and decided to do it the same way one night, only to find that it hurt. Later after my two room mates had stopped laughing, John explained that it was best to wet the ends of your fingers first.

John was always interested in electricity and went on to become a hospital electrical engineer, after serving an apprenticeship at Pontypool Nylon Factory. The building is easily recognisable to me, because it was pointed out to me in the distance whenever it was seen out of the car or train window. "Look!" they would shout "That's where John works," thinking that a young boy would be interested in seeing the building where his cousin worked. Nevertheless it was the custom to point it out to me whenevever we drove past it, going or coming. At least on the way there it indicated being near the end of what seemed an endless journey.

The Nylon Factory at Pontypool

One side effect of John's interests was the fact that he built himself a crystal radio set, and after we were in bed, he would spend a great deal of time trying to tune into Radio Luxembourg.

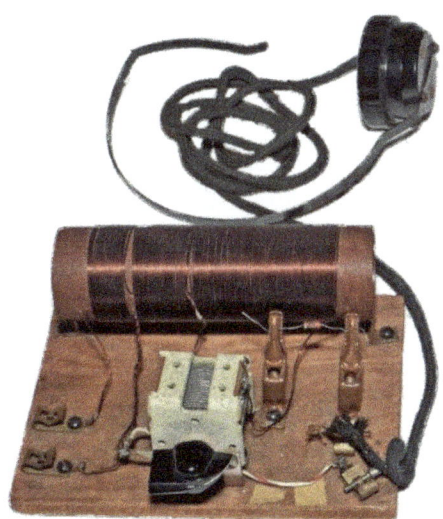

Crystal radio set similar to the one John built

However, a crystal set was actually not very good and required headphones to listen to it, so he very soon invested in a portable battery powered radio of the type show overleaf. I remember how careful we had to be to tune to exactly the right wavelength, and the strength of the signal was reliant on the orientation of the set itself.

At the back of the house was a small square walled yard, where the three of us would play ball games. One side of the yard was of course the back of the house, opposite which was a tall brick wall, the other side of that wall the ground much higher, and slopped gradually away to the mountain behind the house.

To the left was the scullery of the house and the outside toilet. Between the two was a gate leading into the lane that we referred to as "the gully" and gave access, after a turn to the left, onto Tilery Street, emerging to the left of number 18. To the right was the boundary wall of the old Wesleyan Church next door.

Portable Radio

There was only a small gap between the church building and the wall, so if a ball ever went over, I being the smallest, was lifted upand despatched over to fetch it.

In 1903 it had been decided to have a completely new church constructed on a site just south of the old one, adjacent to Tilery Street, with the old church being used as a school room.

I always looked forward to visiting "Abba" as we called it, maybe because it signalled that Christmas Day was close and we would get presents, but maybe because everything was just so different. The only thing I hated was having to use the outside toilet, where there was always torn up newspaper instead of proper toilet paper. Even the horrible "Izal" paper that we used at home was better than that!

Chapel next to 16 Tillery Street

Maybe it was because my father was adopted, together with the family rift that meant he had very little or no contact with them after he met my mother, he became very close to his inlaws. I can remember overhearing my Nan saying how my father had been like a son to her, not a son-in-law.

My father would do any of the routine maintenance at the house in Tillery Street whenever we visited, and it was he who put electricity in, with my help, replacing my much loved gas lights.

That is how I learnt to wire a lighting circuit, including a two-way switch for the stairs. I was small enough to go through the small door into the loft space with a torch. Once up there, my father would make a hole in the ceiling where he wanted the ceiling rose to go, and another where he wanted the switch cable to come down.

Being very dark in the loft, I would quickly spot a ray of light where the holes were. I would pass down the end of a roll of cable, feed it back to the hole for the switch for that room, then cut another lenght to the next room and repeat the process. This was in the days before the loop-in system eliminated the need for separate junction boxes, so it was my responsibility to connect the various cables in junction boxes in the loft, creating a lighting circuit with a switch.

Whenever we moved house we invariably had to rewire the property with the new plastic insulated cable and fittings. The old fabric covered copper wire was prone to start a fire if short circuited, and was housed in wooden conduit to protect it from being chewed by mice or rats.

I've always thought the the British colour code of red for the live cable, black for negative and green for earth that we used, was far more intuitive the the European code of brown for live, blue for negative and striped yellow and green for earth that we were forced to adopt, but don't get me started!

When I drove over to see my cousin John, we would sometimes go to the Rolling Mill pub to see if Uncle Jake was there, and it was on one of these occasions that I heard the locals telling John about an infamous murder enquiry in 1921.

Out with the old (top) and in with the new (bottom)

Apparently, 8-year-old Freda Burnell, was murdered on 5th February 1921. She had last been seen by her father, at approximately 9 o'clock that morning, having been sent on an errand from her home at 9 Earl Street to purchase poultry spice and grit from Mortimer's Stores in nearby Somerset Street to feed the family livestock.

The police arrested and charged a local 15 year old shop assistant, Harold Jones, who worked at the shop. However, Jones was acquitted at Monmouthshire Assizes, despite the evidence presented at this trial, which clearly indicated that Burnell had most likely been killed in the shed belonging to Jones's employers, and that only Harold and the Mortimer family had access to the key.

After deliberating for over five hours the jury found Jones not guilty of the murder, returning a unanimous verdict.

Jones walked free from the courtroom to a private and reportedly tearful reunion with his parents before being escorted to a local restaurant for a meal.

He subsequently returned to Abertillery in a charabanc adorned with flags and bunting to cheers from the local public, most of whom found the notion that a 15-year-old boy could sexually assault and kill a child simply inconceivable.

One of those to greet Jones upon his return was a neighbour named George Little, who greeted him with the statement: "Well done, lad. We knew you didn't do it."

Just over two weeks later, he murdered the man's daughter, 11 year old Florence Little. Jones pleaded guilty to Little's murder and also confessed to having murdered Burnell at his second trial. Sentenced to life in prison because at 15 he was too young to be hanged, he was released in 1941 and moved to London.

Some investigators and authors have suggested that Harold Jones was also likely to be the perpetrator of the Hammersmith nude murders, a series of murders of prostitutes committed between 1964 and 1965 in West London. These theories were only voiced since his death however, and Jones was never considered as a suspect in these murders by the police investigating them.

Harold Jones was giver a pocket watch after his acquittal for the murder of Freda Burnell

Somerset Street Abertillery from where Freda Burnell disappeared

In 2001, reformed gangster Jimmy Tippett, Jr. claimed that, during research for his book about London's gangland, he had uncovered information suggesting that British light heavyweight boxing champion Freddie Mills was responsible for the murders. According to Tippett, Kray-era gangsters, including Charlie Richardson and Frankie Fraser, had long suspected Mills of being the murderer.

Mills had previously been linked with the murders by Peter Neale, a freelance journalist from Balham, south London, who told police in July 1972 that he had received information, in confidence, from a serving chief inspector that Mills "killed the nude prostitutes." He also said that this was "common knowledge in the West End, where many people, if asked would say, "Oh, Freddie did them in."

Mills was found shot dead in his car, apparently by suicide, in July 1965. There were no more killings after his death and the police stopped investigating.

Chapter 4

Conversations about the War

I'm not sure when I first had a real conversation with my father about what he did in the war, but it most probably came about when I asked about the strange looking brass clock in our kitchen, an impression of which is shown here.

Image of our old kitchen clock

I was told that it was from a crashed World War Two bomber, and that my father had managed to get it working again and had made a brass stand for it after the war. In fact, the workshop my father built in the garden of 59 St Michael's Hill was full of intriguing relics from the war.

I can distinctly remember an air raid warden's helmet hanging on a wall, a deactivated hand-grenade mounted on a wooden base, a gas mask, a commando knife and a bayonet, and an air raid siren that could burst an eardrum when you turned the handle. There was also a gas rattle, used to warn of a gas attack, and were often seen at football matches after the war, then referred to as football rattles.

I also seem to remember a strange looking thing rather like a diver's helmet. It was only later that I realised it must have been a gas mask for my brother when he was a baby.

The war had only been over a few years, and artifacts were all around us, some of which were very useful. Like the very tall pair of wooden steps, that I suppose my father must have brought home when he finished working for the Bristol Aeroplane Company after the war.

The baby would pe placed inside the mask during a gas attack

I imagine they were used to reach high places when repairing aircraft, and were not my father's decorating steps as they were then described to us.

My suspicions were due to the impressed Air Ministry stamp on the back, the initials A M and a crown, marking them as property of the Air Ministry

My father was selling second hand furniture from his shop in Alma Vale Road and employed an upholsterer who we all called "Pop". He would recover upholstered items, both to be sold in the shop and as a service to customers. It was from Pop that my father learnt basic upholstery.

Most of the furniture I remember from that time was the furniture in our house. It was utility furniture from the war and was stamped with the utility logo, two capital 'C's' and the figure 41, for "Controlled Commodity 1941" (which soon became known as "the two cheeses") for obvious reasons, see next page. The same logo was used for the utility clothing scheme.

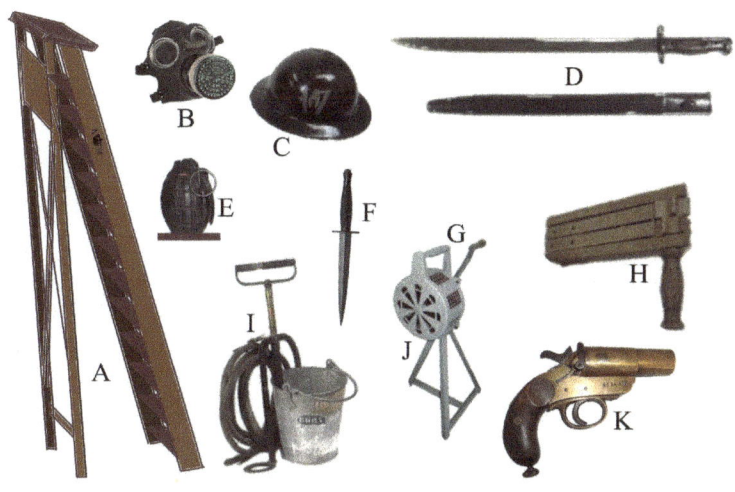

A Air Ministry steps used to reach the top of Aircraft wings for repairs
B Civilian gas mask
C Air Raid Wardens Helmet
D Bayonet
E deactivated hand-grenade
F Commando knife
G Air-raid siren
H Gas attack rattle
I Fire watch stirrup pump
J For incendiary bombs
K Trench signal pistol

Items I can remember seeing in my father's workhsop

In my generation, it was taken for granted that boys would wear short trousers until senior school. I didn't realise at the time that this was part of the governments scheme to save material during the war years.

New furniture was rationed and was restricted to newly-weds and people who had been bombed, under the "Domestic Furniture (Control of Manufacture and Supply (No 2)) Order 1942" operative from 1st November 1942.

The (two cheeses) logo used for utility furniture and clothing

Some examples of utility furniture

My father was never one to miss an opportunity, so if I heard him say that he was going to make some beds, I knew it didn't mean the same thing as when my mum said it.

Mattresses at the time were not sophisticated with box-sping interiors, although some could be found with a coil spring interior, they were mostly stuffed with flock or horsehair and deep buttoned to keep it all in place, and it was the bed-frames that were sprung. Bed irons would bolt onto the head and foot boards (as shown in the drawing) and a sprung frame would sit on top. Sometimes the sprung bed frame itself would incorporate them and bolt on directly, without the need for separate irons.

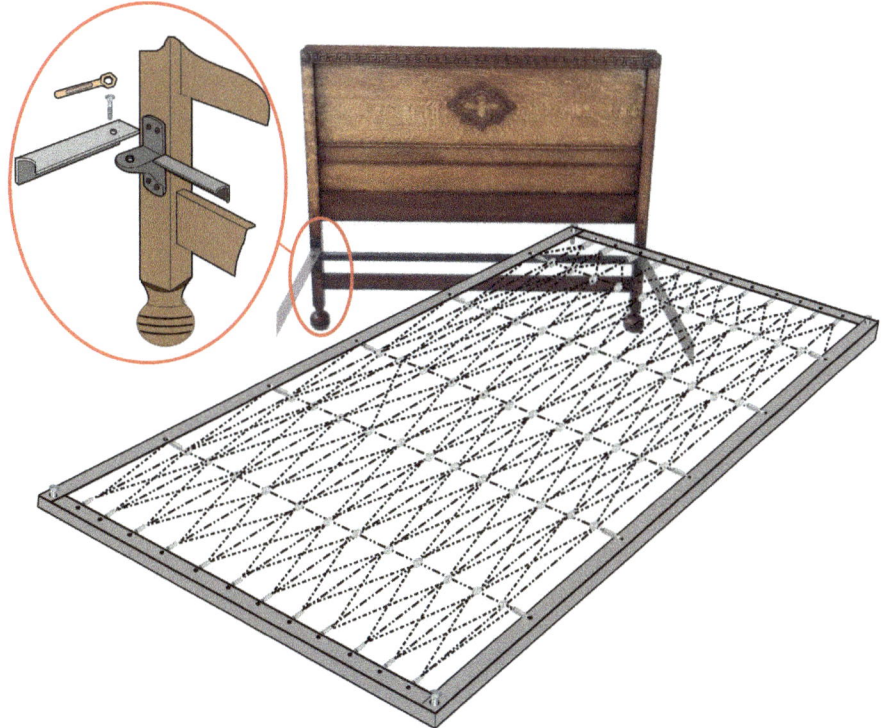

Bed frames would sometime rest on the bed irons and sometomes incorporate them bolting onto the head and foot boards direct

Either way some kind of protection like a blanket was needed, to protect the mattress from being damaged by the metal springs, and a spanner was required to take the bed apart. We were never without a bed spanner. It was an essenstial tool for any furniture dealer, if only because the angle iron was useful in so many different ways. They made good lintels over doors and windows and anything else that needed strong support or reinforcing. My father always had a supply in his workshop in case he needed some for building work.

My father saw an opportunity to provide cheap divan beds that he made himself. He already had a trade account with "Taylors," where he bought the upholstery materials for "Pop", and a builder's merchant for timber, so he manufactured single divan bases in the back yard of 59 St Michael's Hill, and I would be his assistant.

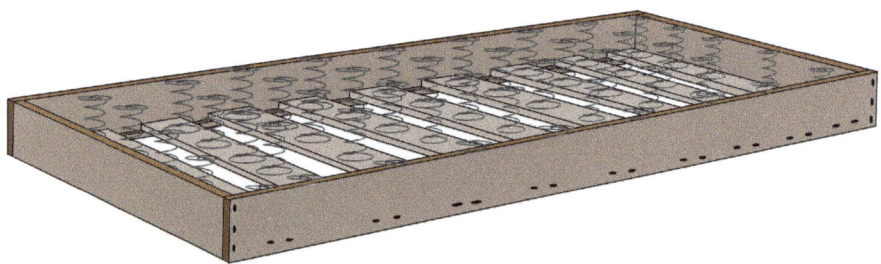

Basic divan base before being upholstered

On trestles we would use 7" X 1" floorboards to make a rectangular frame with slats across the bottom. Staples would secure coil springs in place, and just as in a chair seat, webbing would be interwoven though the springs and stretched taut to compress the springs, which were then sewn in place. Hessian was then pulled over to cover the base followed by a layer of flock and the upholstry ticking befor the base was buttoned.

The 2" X 2" corner blocks that were glued and screwed in place to stengthen the base, were left to project down below the frame and became the legs. The bottom of the legs could then be finished with the Domes-of-silence

The end result with a new mattress and custom made wooden headboard

(furniture glides) and polished or painted. Customers could purchase a new headboard, or they could have one made by dad in wood that they could then paint, or they could have "Pop" cover it in material. The end result looked very professional.

The shop my father ran his business from in Alam Vale Road

You may think that I'm exaggerating the number of bomb sites still undeveloped in Bristol at the time, but the truth is that Bristol is very much the forgotten victim of the Blitz.

Everybody knows that London and Coventry suffered terribly, but the raids on Bristol were never reported as such, due to censorship at the time. The devastating attacks that destroyed large areas of the city centre were reported in the newspapers simply as, "an air raid on a city in the South West."

In truth, Bristol was the fifth most heavily bombed British city in World War Two, with as many as 90,000 buildings destroyed or later declared unsafe and demolished. Among them, were some historic and much-loved buildings and churches. These included the timber framed Dutch House, that was constantly being spoken of.

The Dutch House befor the war

The Duch House was so badly damaged it had to be demolished
Bristol City Archives Ref: 41969/1/67

Bristol was targeted mainly because of its docks and the Bristol Aeroplane Company's plant at Filton and Parnell Aircraft company in Yate.

The first raids on Bristol were in November 1940, during which over 200 people were killed and hundreds of buildings destroyed. St Peter's Church, Castle Park, where my parents were married in 1939, is now maintained as a monument to the civilian war dead of Bristol.

I was born after the end of war and never saw the Dutch House myself, or saw first hand an air raid, or even a bomb site until it had been cleared and made safe, I have however spoken to family, and read and seen many documentaries describing what others who lived through them had experienced.

One programme in particuler featured first hand accounts about the Bristol Blitz and was titled, "The night the sky rained fire". Witnesses described the area around Castle Street and Bristol Bridge as a fire storm. A firestorm is a conflagration of such intense heat that it generates and sustains its own wind system and sometimes occurrs naturally in bush or forest fires. However, they can be also be started by the intense use of incendiary bombs on urban areas, which is documented to have happened in Coventry and Dresden during raids. Unless you've witnessed it personally, I don't suppose its possible to imagine the terrifying sight of flames swirling like gusts of wind, traveling down a street and engulfing everything in its path.

The longest of the Bristol raids was on the night of the 3rd to the 4th January 1941. This was the night the Luftwaffe dropped the largest bomb in their arsenal. Nicknamed "Satan" it weighed 4,400 lb. Fortunately, it failed to explode, and lay undiscovered until April 1943, over two years later, and when the bomb disposal team arrived, they had to dig down 29 feet to get to it; brave men indeed.

Men of course, were not the only ones to show courage during the blitz.

Satan being recovered from Beckington Road, off St John's Lane 1943. (Bristol Archives)

One report concerned two nurses from the Bristol Maternity Hospital. It made national headlines two months later when it was announced that they were to be awarded the George Medal, the second-highest civilian decoration for bravery after the George Cross.

Assistant Matron Elsie Stevens and Sister Violet Frampton volunteered to go out to attend a heavily-pregnant woman at a house nearby just after the air raid siren sounded. They braved falling bombs to find that the patient was trapped in the cellar of a house which was in danger of collapsing.

Stevens was lowered through a narrow opening and crawled through fallen masonry, and with the help of the rescue squad was able to get two children and an elderly woman out. The pregnant woman, though, was completely trapped.

Frampton returned through the blazing streets to get morphine from the hospital, and when she returned she once again went down to give the woman a painkilling injection.

All this was going on during an intense air raid, with bombs falling even some streets away, any one of which could have caused the building they were under to collapse on top of them.

At the same time, they were breathing in coal gas from a broken main. To give support to her brave collegue, Sister Frampton was lowered down as well, and the two of them worked carefully to try to release the trapped woman. It was 3am before they had freed the woman's head and were able to make her slightly more comfortable with sips of tea while the rescue squad desperately worked to free them.

The records and news reports gloss over the details, but it appears that the poor woman gave birth at around 8am. and was only finally freed at 1pm and taken to the hospital, where it was reported that mother and baby were doing well.

Further raids followed, including the one on the 25th April 1941, intended for the Aircraft works at Filton, but the bombs were dropped by mistake on Brislington, Bedminster and Knowle. The last raid occurred on May 15th 1944.

Apart from St Peter's Church, bombs also hit St Mary le Port on 24th November 1940. All that remains of the church is the 15th-century tower, a Grade II listed building, shown below.

St Mary le Port is said to have been founded in Saxon times after Anglo-Saxon foundations were found during archaeological excavations, and Saxon pottery was found nearby. It was located on St Mary le Port Street, an important thoroughfare linking the area around St Peter's Church and later Bristol Castle, High Street, Wine Street and Broad Street. The church was rebuilt and enlarged between the 11th and 16th centuries. The other church shown in the picture, with a copula tower is, All Saints Church in Corn St.

There are plans to develop the site and reinstate St Mary le Port Street.

St Mary le Port Church Tower (left) Tower seen to the right of the damaged buildings is All Saints Church, in Corn Street
Bristol City Arcives: ref 39864/2/469

The principal entrance to All Saints was on Corn Street and the present west entrance is Victorian. When Thomas Paty rebuilt the House of the Guild of 1782, he also rebuilt the remaining north wall of the aisle (shown over the page) squeezed between the tower and Paty's Coffee House.

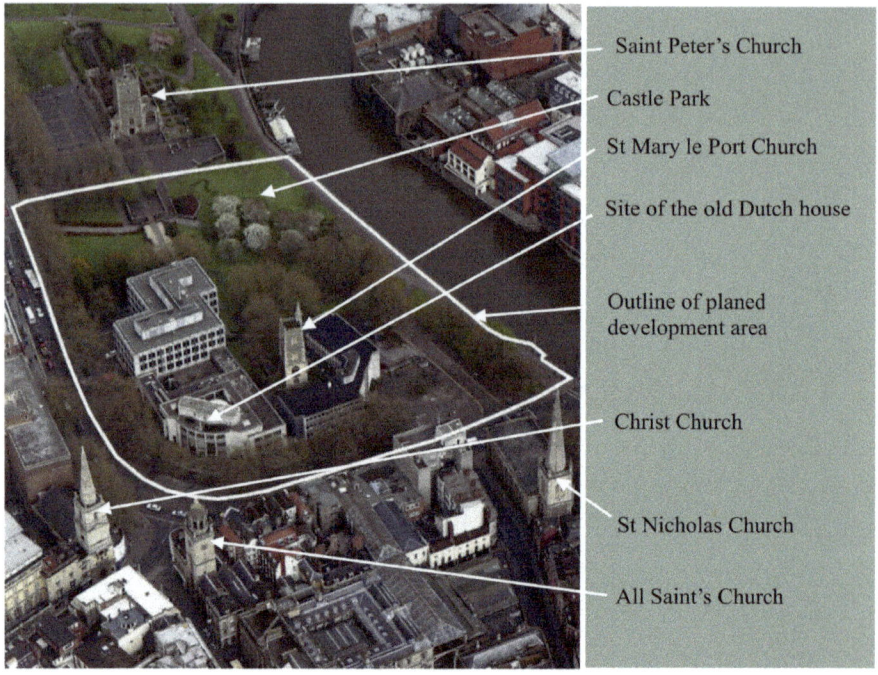

Planned redevelopment of the St Mary le Port area outlined in white

North wall of the aisle

When I was younger, I must have walked along Corn Street a hundred times and never noticed how different that wall looked to the buildings either side.

The Guild of Kalendars was Bristol's most ancient religious guild, existing for at least four hundred years from the twelfth century until the Reformation. It gathered together the clergy and leading citizens for monthly celebrations of the dead in the church of All Saints. From 1464 the guild also operated Bristol's first public library.

Another historic Church that was almost lost completely was, Temple Church, also known as Holy Cross Church. A free-standing bell tower seems to have existed until the early 15th century, on a site further to the west. The present leaning west tower was built in stages, and completed between 1441 and 1460. The highest stage is at a different angle to the vertical of the lower stages, as the masons attempted to correct it because of the subsidence of the lower stages. The top of the tower leans 1.64 metres (5 ft 5 in) from the vertical. It is 114 feet (35 m) high. The lean is popularly attributed to the foundations of the tower being built on top of wool-sacks but is most likely due to the soft alluvial clay underneath being compressed.

After the main body of the church was gutted during an air raid on night of 24th November 1940, the damage was severe and although the arcades, (a range of arches that separate the nave from side aisles) still stood, they were very unsafe and have since been removed.

The wrought-iron screens in the side chapels did survive and are today in the Lord Mayor's Chapel. The sword rest by William Edney is now preserved but broken up into sections and re-erected in other churches. The 15th century candelabrum, with its central statue of the Virgin Mary, also survived, albeit a little dented, and now hangs in the Berkeley Chapel of Bristol Cathedral. Temple Church also contained a peal of 8 bells, which were moved to the Cathedral's north-west tower after the bombing. The bombing also destroyed the stores of valuable historical records kept in the cellars.

Temple Church and leaning Bell Tower

As was usual practice after a raid, buildings that had not been completely destroyed were assessed, to see if they needed to be pulled down to make the site safe. Bristolians often tell of their horror at seeing preparations for the still-standing tower of Temple Church to be demolished, and the lengths they had to go to in order to persuade the demolition teams that the tower was perfectly safe, and that it had been leaning like that for hundreds of years.

Fortunately, the Normandy landings on the 6th June 1944 (D-Day) quickly overran the launching sites of the V1 and V2 rockets that were being prepared, and thankfuly as a result, no rockets were targeted towards Bristol.

One reminder of the Bristol raids can still be seen in the grounds of St Mary Redcliffe Church. A large bomb exploded, and sent a tramline high into the air over houses and eventually impaled itself in the grounds of the Church. The tramline was left where it landed and a plaque added as an explanation.

The plaque reads:

The Plaque in the grounds of St Mary Redcliffe Church

"On Good Friday 11th April 1941 This tramline was thrown over the adjoining houses by a high explosive bomb which fell on Redcliffe Hill. It is left to remind us how narrowly the Church escaped destruction in the war, 1939- 1945"

When I was first told about the plaque by my father, Alan Pegler and myself went to look for it, and found that the tramline and plaque can be viewed easily through the railings at the back of the grounds, from the pavement.

St Mary Redcliffe Church itself was constructed from the 12th to the 15th centuries, and it has been a place of Christian worship for over 900 years. The Grade 1 listed building with its Gothic architecture was reputedly described as "the fairest, goodliest, and most famous parish church in England" by non-other than Queen Elizabeth 1 on her visit to Bristol.

Although a small amount of the 12th century fabric remains, the vast majority of the current building dates from the 13th and 14th century when the building and decorations were paid for by the wealthy merchants of the city, such as Simon de Burton, Mayor of Bristol, and William I Canynges, merchant, five times Mayor of Bristol and three times MP. In the 15th century Canynges' grandson, the great merchant William ll

Canynges, also five times Mayor and three times MP, assumed responsibility for bringing the work of the interior to completion and filling the windows with stained glass, and his tomb and monuments decorate the interior of the church.

The spire fell after being struck by lightning in 1446, and the church remained without one until 1872 when it was rebuilt. The tower contains 14 bells designed for full-circle English-Style change ringing, and the Harrison & Harrison organ provides music for the Choirs. Unfortunately, the English Civil War saw most of the original stained glass destroyed, so most of what can be seen today dates from the Victorian period.

After the bombing of Coventry in 1940, attempts were made to draw attacks away from major cities by building decoy sites nearby, that were made to look like major cities under blackout from the air. Flickering lights were designed to mimic railway marshalling yards at night.

The main decoy sites for Bristol were some 15 miles southwest of the city at Black Down, with another at Chew Magna, but it would seem that these sites were not effective enough to save many of Bristol's historic sites.

Of course, Bristol is such an old city, that many of its historical buildings have been lost as a result of urban development, and the sometimes blinkered vision of town planners, both pre- and post-war, rather than any action by the Luftwaffe. One example to which I draw attention here, is the birthplace of Thomas Chatterton opposite the front of St Mary Redcliffe, and unnoticed by many a Bristolian. The school was demolished in 1939 to widen Pile Street into Redcliffe Way, but the façade was rebuilt on the line of the former back wall.

Thomas Chatterton's place of birth and school. The wall at the right of the house where Chatterton was raised is that of the school c. 1739, where Chatterton's father was master.

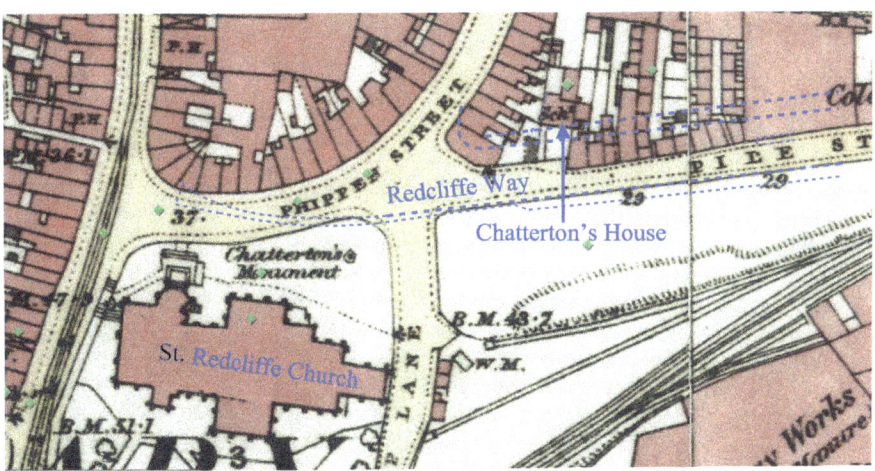

Pile Street was widened to become Redcliffe Way

He was born where the office of sexton of St Mary Redcliffe had long been held by the Chatterton family. The poet's father, also named Thomas Chatterton, was a musician, a poet, a numismatist, and a dabbler in the occult. He had been a sub-chanter at Bristol Cathedral and master of the Pile Street free school, near Redcliffe church.

After Chatterton's birth (15 weeks after his father's death on 7th August 1752) his mother established a girls' school and took in sewing and ornamental needlework. Chatterton himself was admitted to Edward Colston's Charity, a Bristol charity school, in which the curriculum was limited to reading, writing, arithmetic and the catechism.

Thomas however, had always been fascinated with his uncle the sexton and the church of St Mary Redcliffe. He became familiar with the knights, ecclesiastics and civic dignitaries on its altar tombs, before becoming interested in the oaken chests in the muniment rroom over the porch on the north side of the nave, where parchment deeds, as old as the Wars of the Roses, lay forgotten.

From his earliest years, he was liable to fits of abstraction, sitting for hours in what seemed like a trance, or crying for no reason. His lonely circumstances helped foster his natural reserve, and to create the love of mystery which exercised such an influence on the development of his poetry. When Chatterton was age 6, his mother began to recognise his capacity; at age 8, he was so eager for books that he would read and write all day long if undisturbed; by the age of 11, he had become a contributor to Felix Farley's Bristol Journal.

After his confirmation he began to write some religious poems published in that paper. In 1763, a cross which had adorned the churchyard of St Mary Redcliffe for over of three centuries was destroyed by a churchwarden. The spirit of veneration was strong in Chatterton, and he sent to the local journal on 7 January 1764 a satire on the parish vandal.

After moving to London and while walking in St Pancras Churchyard in August 1770, deep in thought, Chatterton failed to notice a newly dug open grave in his path, and tumbled into it. On observing this event, his walking companion helped Chatterton out of the grave, and told him in a jocular manner that he was happy in assisting at the resurrection of genius. Chatterton replied, "My dear friend, I have been at war with the grave for some time now." Chatterton committed suicide three days later.

Having once again digressed enough, I'll return to the aftermath of the war. There was obviously a great shortage, not just of houses, but also of the money and resources to build them. Everybody's expectations were that things would be different to how they had been before the war. Society and the old-world priorities were changing, and there was a Labour government now.

With this new mindset of change, it seems the idea of preserving the past or restoring that which was saveable, took a back seat. The destruction of the city was not looked on by everyone as a burden, but in many quarters it was seen as an opportunity to sweep away the past and build a new, modern, more progressive environment in a new modern style.

Planners must have relished having what must have appeared to them to be a clean slate. They looked at what a lack of planning had produced before; over crowding around dirty factories and a lack of space for gardens or parks.

Unfortunately, the new modern style, with its reinforced concrete and large glass panels took little account of aesthetics. Practicality was all important. Nobody stopped to think about the effect these surroundings, with their concrete and glass facades would have on the communities forced to live amongst them. In fact, most of the mistakes its possible to make, as far as urban regeneration and town planning are concerned, were made in Bristol.

Now I'm no architect, so you may say that I'm not qualified to comment, that I'm simply coming out with the old cliché they use when a non artist criticizes modern art, "I may not know anything about art...but I know what I like." You may be right.

However if you speak to the people who do know and are qualified to criticize, they will agree in most part, and will often cite the redevelopment of Hartcliffe as an example.

I have to point out that things are changing in places like Hartcliffe now, and planners have learned many of the lessons. However back in the late fifties and sixties, with a population of approaching 28,000, it was just too big.

Plenty of flats, but not enough shops, pubs or clubs. Worst of all I'm told, council flats and houses were allocated on a points system, so if you didn't have enough points, you didn't get in. Those who did have enough points were mostly married couples with young children. This meant that the population of these new estates were from the same generation. It was also a time when most young mothers stayed at home as housewives.

With nothing to do except the drudgery of housework and feeding the family, boredom and estate-induced loneliness set in. The children all attended the largest comprehensive schools in Bristol, and when they reached the difficult teenage years, they did it together, and a large number of bored teenagers, with little to do, were bound to become a problem, and crime and drug taking increased.

Hartcille shops built to service the new estate
Bristol City Archives Ref: 40826/StR/164

Most of the population were working class on low wages, but with few shops, the retailers had a captive market, so prices were high and local services poor. To be fair, in the late forties and early fifties, little if any serious research had been conducted into how cities actually work, so I have to admit that in hindsight, it's little wonder that mistakes were made and its far too easy to apportion blame.

Another development that comes to mind is Broadmead shopping centre, now largely replaced by Cabot Circus in another city centre redevelopment.

Before the war it would seem that the main shopping areas of Bristol, essentially made a continuous line of shops all the way from the top of Blackboy Hill, down and along Whiteladies Road and Park Street, to College Green and the City Centre; from there it proceeded along Clare Street, Corn Street, and Wine Street, before continuing along Old Market Street towards Stapleton Road.

According to my parents, if you were shopping for a quality high value item, you would look to Park Street. From there the quality and prices would get cheaper the nearer you got shops near the top of Blackboy Hill, or towards Old Market and beyond, in the other direction. These shops were never part of an overall plan; they didn't all look the same, (thank goodness), they were extentions or add ons to the existing shops. This resulting in an interesting variety of shop fronts and a much better shopping experience.

I have no idea why the town planners decided to build an entirely new shopping centre on the site of the old, admittedly run down, Broadmead area, rather than rebuild on the more war-torn areas, but that's what happened.

Gone: Bruton's piano shop in Broadmead before re-development in 1954. no bomb damage here

Gone: St James's Square Avenue 1954 looking towards Milk St.

I often wonder why so many bueatiful old and structually sound properties have been demolished to make way for new buildings, when there were so many bomb sites that could have been used instead?

Maybe it was just the mind set of the time, or maybe there were good practical reasons for it.

With so many new council houses being built with an inside flushing toilet and hot water on tap, it's little wonder that houses such as the one in Somerset Street, (where Eileen and her mother lived at the time,) with no bathroom and the only source of hot water being a kettle, were declared unfit for human habitation. They were re-housed to a council house in Cadbury Heath. Those houses that were not pulled down would have been provided with a modern hygenic kitchen and bathroom like the one shown here.

Example of a modern council house kitchen

When I first started venturing into town, it was with friends from school. After all, the city centre was only two minutes from St Michael's Hill, where I was living, and St Michael's School we were all attending. We only had to cross Upper

Maudlin Street, descend some steps into Colston Street and we were at the top of Christmas Steps. I never gave it any thought at the time, but just by the top of the steps in Maudlin Street was a curious little building that I later discovered was a signal box for the trams.

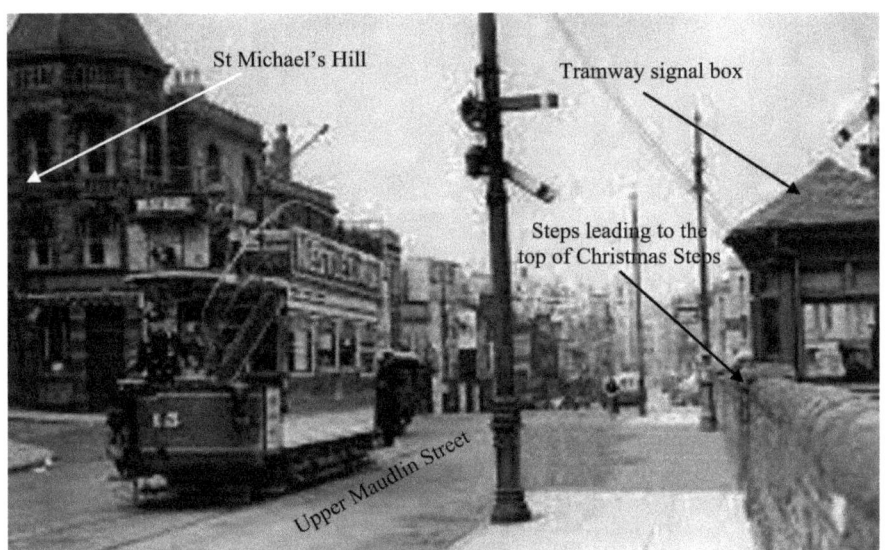

Tramway signal box I remember is no longer there.

If we turned left onto Upper Maudlin Street, past the BRI (Bristol Royal Infirmary) and then turned right into Lower Maudling Street past the Eye and Dental hospitals, we would emerge onto The Horsefair, where the Lewis's Department Store was being built as part of the new development.

If I didn't go with friends, then expeditions into town were with my mother, usually to buy school uniform at Peters in Old Market. The general shopping was done in the local shops at the top of St Michael's Hill, or on Blackboy Hill if I needed new shoes, which would always come from Lennards Shoe shop. There they sold Clarks shoes in different width fittings, and they would measure children's feet accurately.

Lewis's Department Store under construction

Peter shop in Old Market Street 1955

Peters shop in Old Market was a fascinating shop. I remember it selling not just clothes, but also fishing tackle and sub-aqua equipment.

It also had a central cashier and a pully system for delivering the cash from the sales desk to the cashier, who would then send back a receipt and any change in the same way.

Cash delivery system similar to the one I remember

I think we must have caught a bus some of the way, but nevertheless it was a laborious day for a six-year-old.

The Bristol I remember during those outings was one of old looking buildings, with no two looking exactly the same, and the odd gap here and there where a building used to stand. To see the side wall of a building supported with large wooden buttressing and having the remains of a fireplace where a second floor would have been, was just common place to me.

Even in the image above of Peters shop in Old Market, the advertising bill board hoarding to the left of H N Raselle Ltd is covering an undeveloped bomb site.

I suppose in common with most other cities, the Bristol I remember was built up gradually over time, with bits being added over the years. These new bits, were sometimes designed to blend in, but often reflected a new fashion or building material.

The most obvious examples of which are Georgian houses that had their extensions designed and built in the latest Victorian style

This was unlike the new city centre and new housing estates being built to replace what was destroyed in the bombing, which was all in the one new modern style, making it difficult to tell one from another.

Chapter 5

Bristol City Centre as a Port

Although most ships used Avonmouth Docks after the Royal Edward Dock was opened in 1908, ocean-going cargo ships were regularly loaded and unloaded at the City Docks until the 1960s.

In 1972 the Royal Portbury Dock was opened, and the City Docks were finally closed. The harbour buildings, including the tobacco warehouses, became redundant. It was the end of an era.

Bristol is situated on the river Avon six miles inland from where it flows into the Severn Estuary, at the most downstream point where it was convenient to cross the Avon, and where sailing ships could be carried up to the city's harbour on the tidal current of the river. This was both an advantage and a disadvantage for sailing ships. On the plus side, ships could be carried all the way to Bristol docks on the current before the tide changed. On the down side, they would be stranded in the mud when the tide went out. Until the late 1700s, this was not considered too much of a problem, because ships were built to cope with this type of grounding and local pilots would know the best places for ships to "Take the Ground".

Ship "taking the ground" waiting for the next tide.

By the 1760s, however, Bristol was so popular as a destination for cargo ships that it became impossible to accommodate them all, and ships were beginning to use other ports like Liverpool, where there was more capacity. Something had to be done.

Ever since we moved to St Michael's Hill and I started school, I'd heard various terms and phrases such as "the feeder, the rocks railway, box tunnel, plimsol line and floating harbour," and I had no idea what any of them referred to until much later. The floating harbour was the most puzzling to me. After all, I'd seen a railway carrying coal and rocks, and I had already had a few plimsol marks, although I called them "daps" not plimsols, and I remember thinking that a floating harbour must be some kind of large raft floating in the water that ships could moor alongside.

Later I discovered that the merchants in Bristol needed to think of ways to make the harbour non-tidal by damming the river. This would allow the ships that were in harbour to stay afloat rather than have to "Take the Ground", hence a "Floating Harbour."

A tidal bypass for the river was dug for 2 miles through the fields of Bedminster. I have heard it said that the new cut was dug out by French Prisoners, but there is nothing I can find to substantiate the claim. Other, more reliable reports state that the cut was started in 1804 by 600 navvies, (navigational engineers,) this number rising to well over 1,000 by the time it was completed in 1809. The £530,000 scheme was approved by Parliament and construction began in May 1804. The scheme included the construction of the Cumberland Basin, a large wide stretch of the harbour in Hotwells where the quay walls and bollards now have listed building status.

The tidal new cut was constructed from Netham to Hotwells, with another dam installed at this end of the harbour. The Feeder canal between Temple Meads and Netham provided a link to the tidal river so that boats could continue upstream to Bath. However, the new scheme required a way to equalise the levels inside and outside the Dock for the passage of vessels to and from the Avon, and bridges to cross the water. Cumberland Basin was built with two entrance locks from the tidal Avon, and a junction lock between the Basin and what became known as the Floating Harbour.

Bridges were built across the cut. Bedminster Bridge, originally known as Harford Bridge, was an iron bridge built by Coalbrookdale. This was replaced in 1883 by the current bridge, and features the cast iron 'rope' handrails which were saved from the original Harford's Bridge. A concrete bridge was built alongside in the 1960s to double the capacity and create Bedminster Roundabout.

This arrangement provided flexibility of operation with the Basin being used as a lock when there were large numbers of arrivals and sailings. The harbour was officially opened on 1 May 1809, and a celebratory dinner was held on Spike

Island for a thousand of the navvies, who had worked on the construction. At the dinner "two oxen, roasted whole, a proportionate weight of potatoes, and six hundredweight of plum pudding" were served, along with a gallon of strong beer for each man. When the beer ran out a mass brawl between English and Irish labourers turned into a riot which had to be suppressed by a Naval press gang.

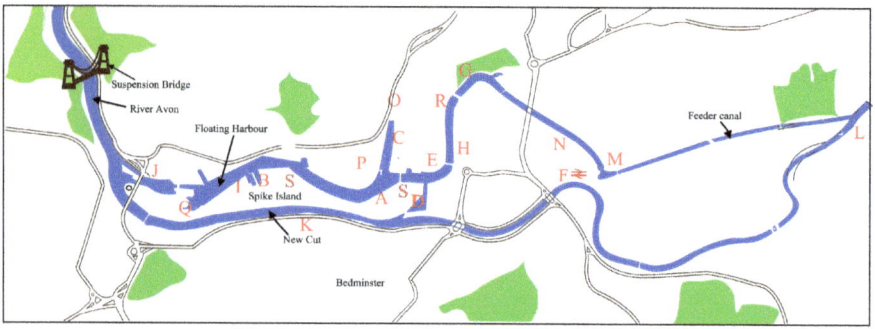

A. Princes Wharf including M Shed
B. Dry docks and SS Great Britain
C. St Augustine's Reach, Pero's Bridge
D. Bathurst Basin
E. Queen Square
F. Temple Meads Station
G. Castle Park
H. Redcliff Quay and Caves
I. Baltic Wharf marina
J. Cumberland Basin and Brunel Locks
K. The New Cut
L. Netham Lock, entrance to Feeder Canal
M. Totterdown Basin
N. Temple Quay
O. The Centre
P. Canons Marsh and Millennium Square
Q. Underfell Yard
R. Bristol Bridge and Welsh Back
S. Patterson's Yards

Floating Harbour

The first vessel built in the Floating Harbour was the Dochfour, but the most famous has to be Brunel's SS Great Britain in 1838. Built at Patterson's Shipyard for the Great Western Steamship Company's transatlantic service between Bristol and New York, she was the first to combine an iron hull and a screw propeller on an ocean-going ship. She was also the first iron steamer to cross the Atlantic Ocean, which she did in 1845, in 14 days.

When launched in 1843, SS *Great Britain* was the largest vessel afloat. But she had taken six years to complete, (1839–1845) and the high cost had left her owners in a difficult financial position. They were forced out of business in 1846, having spent all their remaining funds re-floating the ship after she ran aground at Dundrum Bay in County Down near Newcastle in what is now Northern Ireland, after a navigation error.

In 1852 she was sold for salvage and repaired. Great Britain was later used to carry thousands of emigrants to Australia until being converted to all-sail in1881. Three years later, she was retired to the Falkland Islands, where she was used as a warehouse, quarantine ship and coal hulk until she was scuttled in 1937, 98 years after her keel was laid down.

Scuttled in the Falklands

In 1970, after the ship had been abandoned for 33 years, Sir Jack Arnold Hayward OBE, prominent businessman, developer, and philanthropist, paid for the vessel to be raised and repaired enough to be towed back to the United Kingdom, to be returned to the Bristol dry dock where she had been built 127 years earlier.

Bringing SS Great Britain back from the Falkland Islands to her place of birth in Bristol, where she is now a huge visitor attraction, was no easy matter, and there was worldwide interest. Eventually after being surveyed by naval architects, she was mounted onto a submersible pontoon, "Mulus 111". A German tug ."Varius11", was then chartered and she was towed to Port Stanley to be prepared for the epic transatlantic voyage. Once ready, she was towed to Montevideo for another inspection, before continuing onto Barry Docks, where Bristol-based tugs took over and towed her, still on her pontoon to Avonmouth Docks.

The SS Great Britain was then taken off her pontoon, and now once again truly afloat, she was towed up the River Avon to Cumberland Basin, where she had to wait two weeks for the tide to be high enough to get her through the locks and into the Floating Harbour. I am sure she would have breathed a sigh of relief, as I know many Bristolians did.

Eileen was working at Ham Green Hospital at the time and she walked to where she could see it coming up the Avon, as did many others to witness the historical event.

In 1984 the SS Great Britain was designated as a Historic Mechanical Engineering Landmark. A survey carried out in 1998 discovered that the hull was continuing to corrode in the humid atmosphere of the dock and estimates gave her 25 years before she corroded, so further extensive conservation work was carried out. This included the installation of a glass plate across the dry dock at the level of her water line, with two dehumidifiers, keeping the space beneath at 20% relative humidity. This work being completed, the ship was opened to the public in July 2005, and visitor access to the dry dock was restored. The site is visited by over 150,000 visitors a year with a peak in numbers in 2006 when 200,000 people visited.

I can't help but see the similarity in the two events shown here, photographed with Brunel's Suspension Bridge as a backdrop, the returning of the SS Great Britain to Bristol, and the Concorde returning to Filton. There is a great deal of pride in

Bristol's Aviation, Maritime and Engineering Heritage, despite all the negative press that Bristol seems to attract.

Crowds wacthing the SS Great Britain returning to Bristol

Concorde returing to Filton for the last time

I was born too late to see ships moored actually in the city centre, but I do remember standing near the statue of Neptune, with my back to the city centre, to see cargo ships being loaded and unloaded. Phillip Pobjoy and I often stood watching the cranes in action.

Statue of Neptune overlooking Bristol City Docks
Bristol City Archives Ref: 39864/2/38

No container ships back then of course, so when we watched the cranes in action, they were lifting pallets loaded with sacks or crates out of the ship's holds, which dockers then moved into warehouses on hand-carts.

Hand-carts, like the ones being used on the docks, and shown here, would now realise a good price in an antique auction, and some of the dealers on programmes such as Bargain Hunt or The Antique Road Trip, would positively drool over them. The cranes on the dockside could lift goods from the hold of a ship, either onto waiting goods wagons, onto the dock side as shown here, or palletes ready to go into E or M shed

Wood pulp being unloaded
Bristol City Archive Ref: 40826/DOC/31

A crate of produce arriving at the City docks
Bristol City Archives 40826/DOC/23

Crane outside E shed with Royal Hotel in Background
Bristol City Archives 93864/2/24

One of the cranes on the docks was a Fairbairn steam crain. I never actually saw one in operation unloading goods, but my interest in aviation led me to the following archive photograph of it in operation, loading parts of a sea-plane onto the deck of a ship.

Parts of the Saunders-Roe Princess flying boat on Canons Marsh prior to being loading onto a ship with the steam crane
Bristol City Archives Ref: 40826/DOC/

Remembering the sights and sounds I encountered watching the goods trains loading at the docks, as well as watching the passenger trains at Clifton Down Station, has reminded me that it was only when Alan and I were playing in Redland Park near the railway station, that we spotted our first diesel train! They soon became a more familiar sight at Temple Meads.

Early Diesel train at Temple Meads

Clifton Down station had been had been a place of adventure ground for me from the early days with Phillip Pobjoy, when we used sneak onto the platform, but somehow it lost its magic with the end of the steam era.

Gas lights added a magical element

No more gas lights on the platforms, no more mountains of coal piled up waiting to be loaded onto the engine tenders, nor more dripping water towers, or that special smell that you only get with steam trains.

Chapter 6

Chandos Rd and Senior school

We moved from St Michael's Hill towards the end of my last term in junior school, to number 6 Chandos Road in Redland. I only remember the timing of the move because, for a short while, I had to walk to school all the way along Hampton Road to the roundabout at the junction with Cotham Road, Cotham Hill and St Michael's Hill.

Drinking fountain at the juction of Cotham Hill and Hampton Road

This was an interesting crossroads, having the Missionary and Theological College on one corner and the Bristol Homeopathic Hospital on another. Set into the curved wall between Hampton Road and Cotham Hill was an old drinking fountain.

It was during the school holidays that Phillip and his family moved away and we lost touch. I became friends with Alan Peglar, whose father was the proprietor of the greengrocers next door, and who being the same age as myself, was also about to start at Bishop Road Secondary Modern School when the new term began.

As I remember 6 Chandos Rd. with the telephone box on the front forecourt

Number six was another interesting property with large basement rooms. The one to the left of the basement stairs had a separate coal cellar that would at one time have had a hatch above for coal deliveries. The basement room to the right had large baker's ovens in the wall. Both basement rooms had windows to let in daylight. The front basement had three obscured glass panes under the shop window facing onto Chandos Road. The back room with the ovens had a large sash window allowing light into the room and a door opening onto a small yard some 4 yards wide and 4 foot deep. There were no steps leading up to the back yard, that was about five foot higher, and unless there had been such steps at an earlier time, I surmise the door was simply access to the yard for clearing away debris and cleaning the outside of the window.

Alan Pegler

Alan and I became close friends over the years and had similar interests, including aircraft. On the opposite side of the road to our homes was a toyshop owned by Mr and Mrs Dawson. As soon as we both had our pocket money on a Saturday morning, we would march over the road together and purchase rolls of caps for our toy guns and plastic Airfix models, mostly of World War Two aircraft, and also the odd battleship and Saturn V rocket.

There is one incident that took place in the back yard of number 6, that I always managed to keep secret from both my brother and parents because it involved fireworks, and I didn't want to be banned from buying them. As far as the fifth of November and fireworks were concerned, I had never seen the attraction of bangers, especially after my encounter with the jumping-jack in the garden of 59. However, every November 5th saw a ready supply of penny bangers available and I wanted to try something out.

Remember that I had been taught to solder by my father, and I wondered if I could use this skill to make my own cannon. I cut off a length of 3/4 inch copper pipe from the stock in dad's workshop, and after flattening one end with a hammer, soldered up the end before bending it over on itself. After then drilling a small "touch-hole," I poured the contents of a penny banger in the open end, followed by a glass marble and a piece of cotton rag that I rammed in place as if loading a musket.

With just a little trepidation, I struck a match and held it to the touch-hole. There was a somewhat disappointing "puff" sound and the marble stayed put.

Surmising that there had not been a tight enough fit between the sides of the marble and the inside face of the pipe, I tried again, this time with a slightly larger marble with a strip of sellotape around it. I actually had to push this firmly into the pipe with a length of dowel rod.

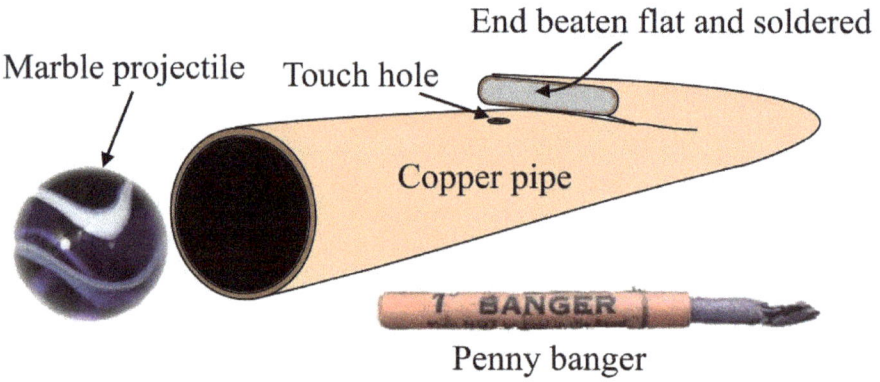

Home made cannon

This time the effect of igniting the powder was far more dramatic, as the marble was apparently too good a fit, and the pipe itself split open, covering the base of my thumb in a very painful powder-burn that took ages to heal.

It was also around this time that my father gave me a German Military Dress Bayonet to hang on my wall. This birthday gift kicked off my interest in collecting antique weapons, and I soon had several bayonets, a dress sword and, a five-shot revolver that we found in a secret compartment of an old bureau that my father had bought.

One of my father's customers, who ran a local garage, was also a collector and restorer of antique guns. He offered me two rather exquisite dress swords in exchange for the revolver, and feeling pressured into doing the swap I accepted After all, the revolver just sat on a shelf in my room, whereas the two swords looked rather splendid on my wall.

Of course, it was early days and I had only just started buying books on the subject of firearms, which later became my real interest, so I didn't realise the importance of the revolver.

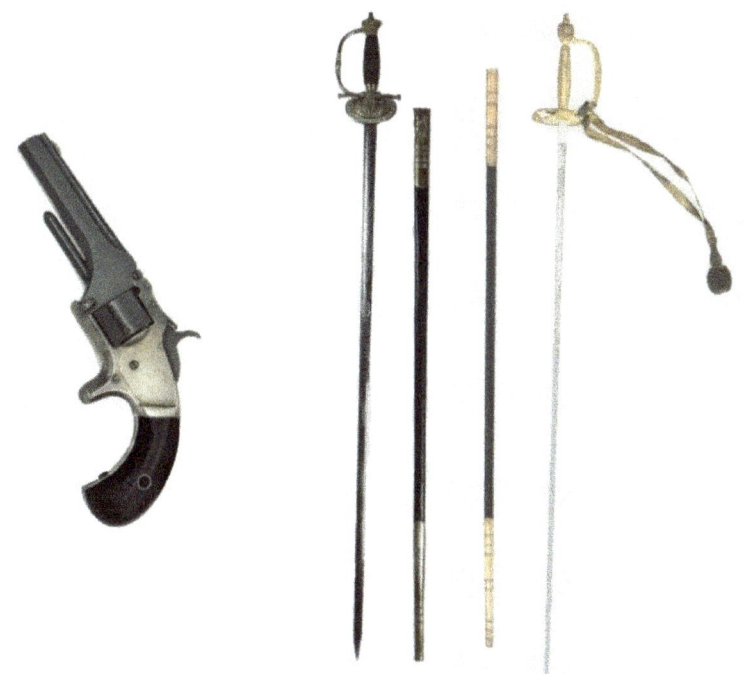

The revolver I exchaned next to the two dress swords

When I became more knowledgeable I regretted my decision. The revolver was an example of a Smith & Wesson five shot rim-fire that was the first gun to have a drilled through cylinder and take the modern self-contained cartridge that had been developed by Smith & Wesson - a landmark in firearms development.

Over the next few years my collection continued to grow. Family and friends all knew that I collected weapons and militaria, so birthday and Christmas presents were never a problem. It even got to the stage where, an elderly neighbour who lived in Cowper Road was moving into a home and needed to dispose of some possessions, he asked my father if I would like his old army .303 rifle.

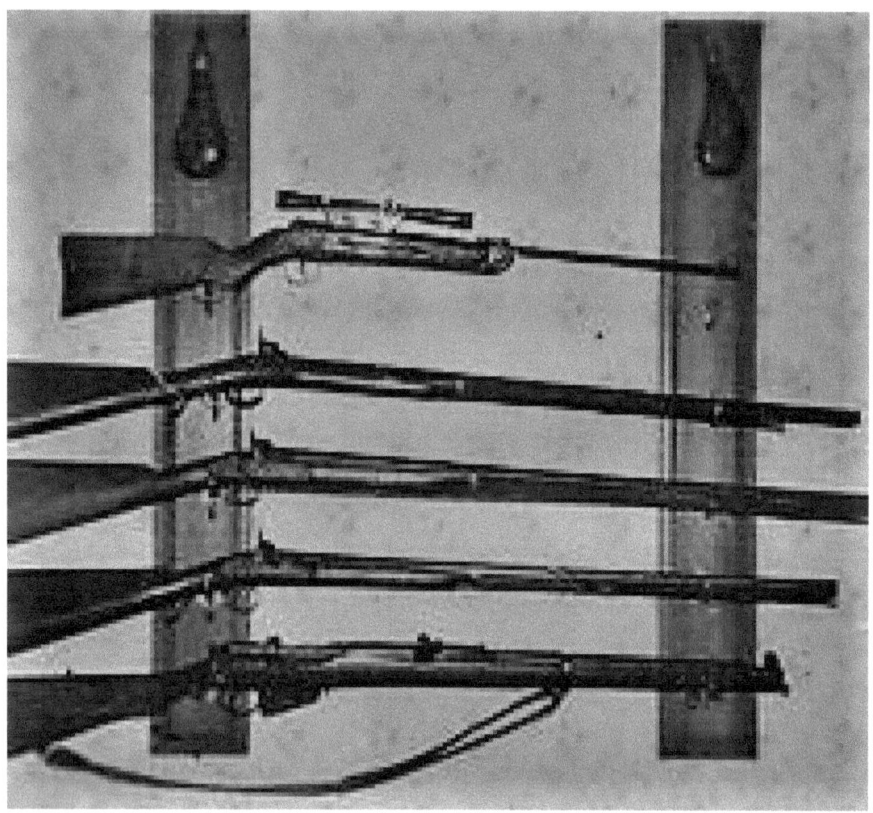

The .303 was displayed with my percussion muskets and air-rifle

I know it probably sounds strange to people now, but back then, Second World War was still in everyone's minds. The pictures Alan and I went to see at the cinema included 633 Squadron, Where Eagles Dare, The Great Escape and The Longest Day, so collecting war memorabilia just seemed normal.

In addition to the items shown here, I possessed, four Nazi

Dress daggers an ensign taken from a German U-boat that had the hated Swastika at it's centre, a couple of Very pistols, a commando knife, several Knobkerries, a Gurkha knife or Kukri, a Javanese Kris, several powder and shot horns, a couple of round shields of unknown origin and a Zulu shield and Assegai. The walls of my bedroom looked more like those of a castle armoury.

The walls of my bedroom looked more like those of a castle

I can't remember exactly what sparked off my interest in photography. Maybe it was because I started to record the odd piece of furniture, but I soon began to lose interest, when others proved far better at it than I. However there was a very brief period when I tried to photograph my collection more artisticallly. You must judge for yourselves whether I should have pursued it further or not, but two of my efforts are show below.

It might have been better to photograph the pistols individually?

During my year in senior school I began playing chess with a few class-mates, and we joined the school chess club. Of course, buying a chess board to play on was never going to suffice for me, so I soon ended up with a Victorian inlaid games table and an antique ivory chess set. Although it was clear that I was never going to become a grand-master, the games table did look good, and provided me with another opportunity to display my pistols collection artistically. It wasn't a good result! You can barely make out the derringer, or the flintlock pocket pistol in the middle of the table. At least it eliminated two possible careers for me to pursue. No photography and nothing that involved planning or strategy. I'd also discoverd by visiting the dentist, that I had a low pain threshhold, so espionage was out as well!

Games table and ivory chess-set , proved a poor background for displaying pistols.

At the age of eleven I started at what was then Bishop Road Secondary Modern School in Bishop Road, and as luck would have it, my new friend Alan was in the same class. The head master, Mr Phillpotts, left after we had been there just the one term and his replacement Mr Biggs, was a very ambitious man who soon had the school's name changed to **Bishopston** Secondary Modern, rather than **Bishop Road,** and introduced a school uniform. He also appeared to be in a position to spend money and soon had new equipment supplied, including a set of fold-out wall bars and ropes for the school Gymnasium.

My time at Secondary School was a turbulent one that started badly, but gradually improved as I got older. The downside was the fact that although I was reading several books a week, my ability to spell was sadly lacking. It became annoying, whenever I had my work marked or my report writen at the end of term, I would always have to face the same comments from teachers, "Colin's spelling is very poor and would be improved by reading more books."

I saw little point in informing them that I had been reading three or four W. E. Johns books a week and had recently discovered Dennis Wheatley. My spelling didn't improve however, no matter how much I read.

As for maths, I wasn't too bad when things were written down, but I was hopeless at mental arithmetic, I could only seem to keep one figure in my head at any one time. Our maths tutor, Mr Owen, a short Welshman who I disliked intensely, would always pick one or two of us to stand up in front of the class, give us a sum to do in our heads, and time us to see how long we took to get the answer. He almost always picked me as one of the ones to be tested, and seemed to take a delight in humiliating me in front of my classmates with remarks like "My God Holcombe! Did you miss a lot of junior school, for some reason?" I dreaded his classes.

I have the same problem even now, if I keep a team scorecard at golf. When we've finished putting, everyone calls out their scores to me, and by the time I get to my bag to record the scores, I've forgotten who had what as well as my own score. I think I must have always had a slight short term memory problem, or maybe Mr Owen was right and I was just thick! I like to blame it either on my mother smoking while she was pregnant with me, or the "Short Wave" treatment I had as a child. Either way, I've coped with it and it hasn't caused me too many problems in my work.

My early teenage years before I left school were reasonably enjoyable, once the teaching staff accepted what I was and wasn't capable of.

Gymnastics was never going to be my thing, and my legs were too short to be a runner, so I was never close to any of the sports staff. Music class seemed to consist mostly of singing, unless you were one of the gifted ones, who could play an instrument as well, so when we entered the music room for a lesson, I was invariably asked if I wanted to go and help Mr Hody in the woodwork shop instead, which I always opted for. I was a win win, the music tutor didn't have to hear we sing, and I think Mr Hody enjoyed having an assistant. I had a good relationship with Mr Hody, as I did with a new English teacher who joined the staff when I was thirteen.

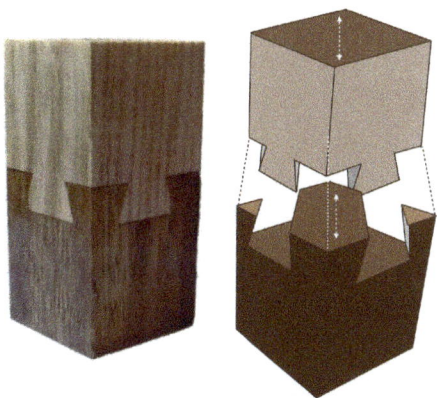
Puzzle dovetail joint

My relationship with the woodwork teacher Mr Hody, stemmed from the time he showed my class how to mark out and cut a dovetail joint, something I was more than proficient at already As the rest of the class made simple dovetails, I sneaked into the wood store and picked out some off-cuts of walnut and oak, determined to show off my skills. Confident, or maybe I should say arrogant enough, to think that Mr. Hody would feel no need to check how I was doing, I made an example of a puzzle dovetail, that I'd been shown. It looks like four dovetails that would be impossible to put together, whereas in fact, it's two sliding dovetails as shown here. He was so impressed with my effort that when one of the other teachers called in to discuss something with him, he insisted on calling me over to show him, and asked him if he could see how such a joint was possible. I realised after, that it had a mistake to show off like that, when some remarks frome other members of my class hit home; you live and learn.

Mr Sabin, the new English teacher, was a strict disciplinarian who was very unpopular with pupils until they got to know him, a process that for some took a couple of months. After those first months however, I believe he became the most popular member of staff, and when he left the term before I did, a large amount of money had been collected for his leaving present, and I believe there were unprecedented numbers of personal tributes and gifts.

My last year at school saw me start to play tennis weekends and snooker in the evenings, it was also the first time I had a regular girlfriend, Anne, a girl in my class who played the violin, and practised with the Bristol Youth Orchestra.

I mentioned earlier that I wasn't very athletic, but I was becoming competitive. When we heard that the girls were going to be allowed to play football if they wanted, and boys could opt for tennis as an alternative to cricket, a few of us were keen to change sport, partly, in my case because I prefered tennis to cricket and was better at it. It had absolutely nothing to do with the fact tennis with the girls seemed like it could be fun. However on the first day, when we were lined up ready to get onto the coaches to take us to the sports ground, Mr Lewis looked up and down the line of boys and said in a kind of sneering voice that sounded full of contempt, "If any of you boys want to play tennis with the girls, step forward now."

I knew that I wasn't the only one who wanted to play tennis, rather than hang around an outfield waiting for a chance to bat or bowl, so I waited to step forward as soon as someone else started the ball rolling. But it seemed that I was not the only one unwilling to be the first. So cricket it was. I was twelve years old however and just begining to find some confidence, both in my ability and standing in school, and also socially. In my last year at school I even started playing tennis on a reguler basis at Ardargh bowls and tennis facilties on Horfield Common. The bowling green and pavilion are some of the settings, along with Henleaze High Street at the heart of the comedy heist movie, "Golden Years".

Ardargh Pavillion

I also started playing snooker and darts with some friends on the way home from school, there being a large snooker hall over Burtons Outfitters on the corner of Elton Road and Gloscester Road. It turned out that my father was also a snooker fan, and used to play at the Vaughan Billiards and

Snooker Club, near Quarry Steps, close to the top of Blackboy Hill. He took me there, unsure if it still existed, and we found that the door was nearly always open; all you had to do was put money in a meter to pay for the lights. It became one of our favorite haunts. My father also bought a quarter size table for our front room.

I was of course studying for my O-level exams at this time and intended taking, English literature, technical drawing, woodwork, geography, general science, and commerce, a new subject introduced that year as an alternative to maths.

I can remember my excitement when Mr Sabin told us that for English, along with, The Cloister and the Hearth, and The Red Badge of Courage, we would be studying an H.G. Wells story and one Shakespeare play. I was hoping for one of the histories such as Richard III or Henry V for the Shakespeare play, together with maybe The Time Machine or The War of the Worlds, from Mr. Wells. In reality, it turned out to be Twelfth Night and The History of Mr. Polly. A huge disappointment that I felt Mr. Sabin shared.

The reason Mr Sabin and I got on well was because of a shared interest in both Science Fiction and collecting firearms. This became apparent when, as part of an English language lesson, he wrote a poem on the blackboard with adjectives missing, and asked the class to suggest some. I just happened to know the poem, The Kraken" by Alfred Lord Tennyson, because it was on the inside page of the book I was reading at the time, "The Kraken Wakes." by John Wyndham. So when asked for a suitable adjectives to fit "Below the ......?.....of the upper deep," and most of my classmates suggested, words such as fathoms, darkness or coldness, I rather smugly suggested, "Thunders."

He called me to his desk after class to ask how I was so familiar with the poem. It transpired that we were both reading the same John Wyndham book, and we had a long chat during which time he explained the meaning of some of the terms and phrases used in the poem, such as "Until the Latter Fire shall heat the deep." which he explained, referred to the end of the world. He also asked me to bring in some photographs of my collection, which I did the next day. It turned out that he had a percussion pistol and wanted to know more about it and whether or not it could be restored.

It's unbelievable, even to me now, but when he learned that I knew a man who restored guns as a hobby, he brought it into school in a sports-bag and I took it home to show the restorer who wrote a report on the gun for me to take back.

The importance of discretion was emphasized by my tutor, who pointed out the possible headlines in the papers if anyone discovered that a school teacher had given a gun to one of his pupils.

Bishop Road School is very close to the walls of Horfield Prison, and during my last full term in December 1963, one of the last men to be hanged in Britain was executed in the grounds of the prison.

Russell Pascoe aged 24 and Dennis John Whitty were both found guilty of murdering 64-year-old William Garfield Rowe at a farm in Cornwall. The two men had believed local gossip that Rowe kept a large amount of money at his farm, and visited the farm to steal it. Things went badly wrong and they ended up murdering Mr Rowe. At trial they were both found guilty and sentenced to be hanged simultaneously at 8 a.m. on Tuesday the 17th December 1963. Side by side hangings had been outlawed in 1957, so Whitty was sent to Winchester prison and Pascoe to Horfield because Bodmin no longer had an execution facility.

Executions in Bristol took place at Gallows Acre at the top of St. Michael's Hill until 1816, and Public Executions were then conducted at New Gaol on Spike Island until 1849, when Bristol's final public hanging took place at the New Gaol.

Servant girl Sarah Harriet Thomas, 19, had been found guilty of killing her elderly employer Miss Elizabeth Jefferies, by bludgeoning her to death in her own bed.

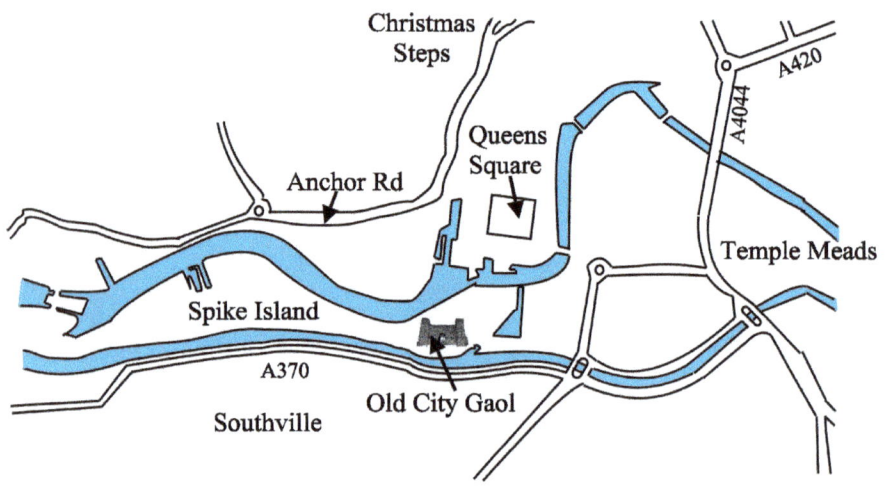

Site of the New Goal on Spike Island

Throughout her trial she had not appeared to treat the court proceedings seriously, but records state that when the Judge put on his black cap and passed sentence she collapsed and broke down completely.

William Calcraft, the longest-serving executioner in England, was contracted to carry out the sentence, but even he was greatly affected by her youth and good looks.

On the day of her execution, Sarah was dragged screaming to the gallows where she continued to sob, scream and plead for her life right up to the final moment, and even the prison governor was so overcome by the scene that he fainted.

A crime reporter at the time, Mr E. Austin, who attended the execution, reported that, although there was the usual drinking and celebrating in the local taverns after the event, a great many of the crowd had felt repulsed by what they had seen, and many carried the memory of that grisly day for years afterwards.

Notice of the public execution of Sarah Thomas

Later that year public executions were prohibited, and they were then carried out behind the walls of Horfield Prison, away from the public gaze.

The death penalty remained a technical option for the punishment of those found guilty of treason until it was finally abolished in 1998.

Although I attended Bishop Road School and realised that it was an old building, I never gave its history much thought. After all, I had spent my life up till then in old and interesting buildings, so why should my school be any different? The school had opened in 1896, and although of no great architectural significance, it is notable for having educated both Cary Grant and Paul Dirac.

In fact, since I learnt that theoretical physicist, Paul Adrien Maurice Dirac OM FRS, who is regarded as one of the most significant physicists of the 20th century (and shared the 1933 Nobel Prize in Physics with Erwin Schrödinger) was educated there, if anybody asks me which school I attended, my answer is now, "The same school as Paul Dirac."

My answer doesn't impress many people however, because few people other than science fiction enthusiasts and followers of Star Trek, have heard of Paul Dirac, the man who predicted the existence of anti-matter, and who even Albert Einstein regarded as a genius. However, when I point out that Cary Grant also attended school there, their interest perks up.

Bishop Road School

In fact there is now a commemerative plaque inside the school, bearing the Dirac Equation.

Plaque bearing the Dirac Equation

In the end I left school before taking any exams, to start an apprenticeship as an, antique furniture restorer, with Hall and Rohan, a firm of antique dealers and restorers based in The Mall in Clifton.

Whether I should have stayed on to take my exams, instead of taking the apprenticeship as my teachers insisted, I shall never know. There have been times when I have regretted not having any formal qualifications, despite ending up with my signed indenture together with a signed letter, certifying that I had completed my apprenticeship and was now a qualified Antique Furniture Restorer.

As it turned out I served my apprenticeship under two interesting, but very different people. Brian Riggs, was a very skilled restorer by day, and a successful magician and cabaret entertainer (The Great Donnelli) evenings and weekends; and Carlo Vasco Perrona, an Italian restorer who you will hear more about later.

I stayed working with Carlo after Brian had left to set up his own business, and after serving a five year apprenticeship became a qualified antique furniture restorer and recieved the following letter in the post along with my indentures .

Hall & Rohan
Antique Furniture
English and Irish Glass
Expert Restorations

LICENSED VALUERS
TELEPHONE
30358/9

The Mall Antique Galleries
Clifton
Bristol 8
BS8 4DS

11th March, 1969.

Dear Sir,

    Now that you have completed your full term of apprenticeship we present you with the enclosed indenture.

    At the same time we certify that having carried out your apprenticeship with diligence and application, you are now competent and qualified in the craft and trade of restorer on antique furniture.

    We hope that our association will continue for many years to come.

                  Yours faithfully,

                    T.A.I. Hall.
                  Director, Hall and Rohan, Limited.

C. Holcombe, Esq.,
6, Chandos Road,
Redland,
BRISTOL, 6.,

DIRECTORS: T. A. I. HALL. J. J. FRY. J. O. HALL

Letter from Hall & Rohan. The nearest thing I have to a qualification

Chapter 7

Holidays

As a family we could never afford to spend money going away on summer holidays. My father was reluctant to close the shop for a whole week, which I think is why we always spent the Christmas break in "Abba," and why if the weather was dry, we would go somewhere after Sunday lunch. The favourite places were Portishead, Clevedon, Weston-s-Mare or Ashton Court Estate (Lady Smyth's as my mother called it.)

Six year old me on the beach at W-s-M, why I'm wearing my school blazer is anybody's guess?

Lady Smyth's offered a chance to give Ricky, our Boxer dog, a good run, and there was lots of room to play ball games such as French cricket or rounders. Clevedon offered the Victorian pier and a amusement arcade with lots of slot machines. I loved to play the tipping point game. Weston had the Grand Pier, a crazy house, dodgems and some fairground rides as well and a sandy beach.

Portishead had a headland with some WW2 gun emplacements, that were interesting to explore, and a boating lake. You could hire paddle boats for the children, small rowing boats for the older ones and skiffs with a fancy seat, so that dads could take the family out on the lake, or teenage boys could try to impress their girl friends by rowing them around the island in the middle of the lake, while they sat smiling in the ornate seat.

Boating lake at Portishead

Once I had outgrown the paddle boats, this presented me with my first experience of rowing, an utterly perverse way of propelling a craft through water.

Whoever thought that it was a good idea to face in the opposite direction to the way you wanted to go, and try to travel in a straight line by applying an equal amount of thrust on both side of the vessel with arms that were clearly always going to be of unequal strength needs his head examined.

I admit that I don't come from a particularly prestigious line of inventors, in fact I believe one of my ancestors is recorded as having said of the horseless carriage, "What's the bloody good of a carriage without a horse!?" But I like to think that even he, like Mr Benz who made the first motor car, would have put the steering at the front and sat the driver facing the way they were intending to go. Why maritime designers, even when they decided to face the front, still put the steering (tiller and rudder) at the back is beyond me. Even horses, not particularly noted for their good sense, would never think of facing the cart and walking backwards! You may realise from my comments that I never considered rowing as a sport.

After the move to Chandos Road my father's business started doing well. He began buying houses and converting them into flats to let out, just as he had done with the upper floors of St Michael's Hill, so when I was about twelve, we had our first summer holiday away as a family.

My father rented a house in Paignton, Devon for a week, two minutes walk from the beach. We played cricket in the garden and visited Torquay and Brixham on days out. We all enjoyed it so much, my father booked again the following year and asked my cousin John if he would like to join us, which he did.

Many of first-time experiences happened when I was with my cousin John. The first time I swam in a river, and my first time on a roller coaster (Barry Island), so it's no surprise that the following year saw me swim in the sea, go mackerel fishing from a boat, and sunbathe on a beach, all for the first time. It was also the first time I'd seen girls sunbathing in bikinis, which was certainly no deterrent to beach holidays for a young lad in the future.

My cousin John pictured with dad and myself in the garden of the rented house in Paignton

Possibly as a thankyou for taking John on holiday to Paignton, I was invited up to stay for a week with John and his mum and dad in Cwncelyn, Blaina, not far from Abertillery. I stayed with and shared a room with my cousin in a small terraced cottage in Quarry Row. Previously they had been living in a prefab not far away, and I believe they were staying in Quarry Row until their council house was ready for them. The houses in Quarry Row had front doors that opened directly onto the road, with not even a pavement outside. Across the narrow road there was space to park a couple of cars, if the people who lived there could afford a vehicle, and a gate that opened into the garden.

My Uncle Jack bred budgerigars at the time, and had an aviary in the garden. One of the things I did during my stay was to feed them in the mornings and top up the water bowls.

My Nan and Granddad alway had a budgerigar in Abertillery, and I remember that it could not only talk, but had a large volcabulary including. "Good boy, Morning Joey, give us a kiss, and Jake's drunk." This last obviously picked up because my Uncle Jake, would often come home from the Rolling Mill, having had too much to drink, and fall asleep on the couch. John and I speculated that his war time experiences in Dunkirk may have been at least part of the reason for his behavior.

There had also been a suggestion that he had been seeing a girl and the family thought that they would get engaged, but that they parted sometime before Jake enlisted, after which he never married.

Some of the houses in Quarry Row

The other great thing about staying there with John, was the fact that at the bottom of the garden was another gate, beyond which was wild countryside and a fast flowing stream.

John called it the feeder, and we would spend hours trying to build dams across it. At one end there was a sluice gate, the other side of which the stream disappeared underground.

I last visited the area many years ago to discover that the landscape of the valleys had totally changed from how I remember it. The slag-heaps that were such a common sight have all gone, and the area I described as wild countryside is now a nature reserve and picnic area.

When I was sixteen, Alan and I decided that it was time we went away together to see the sights of London, so we bought train tickets to the capital and headed off. After arriving we located a small hotel and booked in for three nights. We must have travelled hundreds of miles on the underground after quickly discovering that the underground map, which was so easy to follow, bore no symmetry whatsoever with its surface equivalent.

Nevertheless we not only visited all the main tourist sights, but also managed to visit my relatives Aunty Sis and Uncle Jack who then put us on the train to Bagshot, where Sylvia and Dennis would meet us, and take us to their home in Camberly. We did however manage to catch the wrong train, and had to ring to tell them. Luckily Dennis was very understanding and drove to pick up two red-faced passengers from the station later than expected.

Confident and seasoned travellers after our experiences in London, we booked a B and B in Paignton the following year, both keen to spend sunny days on the beach and swimming in the sea.

Although I described us as confident and seasoned, it soon became apparent that we still had much to learn. When booking the B and B I had explained that we were two lads who would share a room. Not famillier with the subtle difference between the terms double room and twin room, we were a little perturbed to discover that we would be sharing not just the room but a bed as well! We did enquire if we could change rooms, but the accomodation was full. Oh well, if it was OK for Morecambe and Wise.

Things changed considerably when we both passed our driving tests and bought cars. Mine was a 1959 Vaxhall Victor. It was a three gear column change, with bench seats, a fitted radio and I was the envy of all my mates.

1959 Vaxhall Victor

When I first started working for Tony Hall, he employed a driver, being unable to drive himself, as a result of being badly wounded during the war.

His driver, a Mr Whitfield, would also take the Morris Oxford estate-car to pick up or deliver furniture, and if it needed two people he was able to call on me. This was the first time I had seen a large flat "dealers roof rack", custom made to fit any vehicle; they were the roof-rack of choice for antique dealers. It also meant that I soon became more than proficient at securing furniture with ropes to make sure they were safe to transport on top of a moving car without damage.

When Mr Whitfield left the firm he was replaced by Richard, a young man who took the job in order to learn about antiques with a view to becaming a dealer in his own right later on.

Morris Oxford Estate with with a flat roof rack that was a must have for any furniture dealer in the sixties

Richard was much closer to me in age and we became friends. Exactly how Alan, Richard and myself ended up agreeing to tour Wales in my car, I don't know, but we did, and inevitably Richard and I insisted on stopping every time we spotted an antique shop, (well I did have a roof-rack) much to Alan's annoyance.

I think my next holiday must have been the following year because I spent it on a cabin cruiser with Geoffrey Capstick and two friends of his. I think I was invited along because I was the only one with a car, and I remember driving to the Norfolk Broads in the Vauxhall Victor, having first driven down to pick up the fourth member of our party in Southhampton and spending a weekend there with him as guests of his mother. Nevertheless it was a most enjoyable holiday.

Holiday on the Broads

After that it was touring again, this time in Alan's car, a two-tone red and cream Sunbeam Rapier, and by far the sportiest looking car either of us had owned to date. Although not a convertable, there was no door pillar, so with the front windows down the rear window could also be opened, to leave the whole side of the passenger compartment open. We decided to tour all around the coast of Ireland and invited Geoffrey to join us as with another friend from schooldays John Bryant, who was in the Royal Navy and had visited Londonderry before.

On holiday in Ireland

Same colour make and model Sunbeam Rapier as Alan's

John had access to a large frame tent and other camping equipment, so it was decided that we would camp wherever we could. The first night we found a field that looked suitable, but as we were about to start preparing something to eat we spotted two rather large gentlemen in suits and ties marching purposely towards us. We fully expected to be told that it was private land and made to move on. Instead, we were asked what we were doing, and whether we were hungry. After revealing a little more about our holiday plans, we were told that they were dressed in suits because it was their sister's wedding day, and the reception was being held in the large family home, that was just out of sight behind a small copse of trees.

Still unsure why we had been approached, we were then invited over to the house, as there was a great deal of food and drink left over. Our first introduction to Irish hospitality was being invited over to a dining room full of some quite valuable items of silverware, and told to help ourselves, whilst unatended, to as much of the food and *"opened"* bottles of wine and champagne as we liked! Where else would that be likely to happen I wonder?

I've mentioned that Alan shared my interest in aircraft, and we had often talked of becoming pilots. However, the only way we could get the training was to either join the RAF, and hope to get onto the pilot training programme, or pay for private lessons. Flying lessons were very expensive, and depended on the type of plane and the reputation of the tutor. I spoke to a dealer friend of my father's, who I knew was a glider pilot, about the options available to us.

I was informed that in order to be eligible to take the test for a PPL (Private Pilot's Licence) one had to have logged a minimum number of hours in powered aircraft, so the typical cost at that time of getting a PPL was well beyond our means. His advice was to join his gliding club at Aston Down, near Minchinhampton, where the average cost of getting a glider pilots licence, even with club membership and launch fees was much lower, and if you obtained a C certificate in gliding, you would only need a fraction of the number of hours logged in powered aircaft, to take the PPL test. So it would be a much more affordable, if longer process.

"Would it be easy to make the transition from gliders to powered aircraft?" I asked, to which Larry replied, "I've never met a glider pilot who couldn't easily transition to flying a powered aircraft."

Some time later Alan suggested to me that we could go on a gliding holiday, during which we could learn to fly, and he showed me a leaflet he had picked up advertising holidays at Nympsfield, home of the Bristol Gliding Club.

The gliding holiday was an easy decision to make. We were both in paid employment, both had cars, the holiday included full board at a local pub The Rose and Crown, as well as temporary membership of the club and free tuition in the club's gliders. It sounded like the perfect holiday for a couple of aspiring aviators.

The holiday lived up to and even exceeded our expectations. After a very enjoyable and fortunately warm and sunny week, staying with a group of likeminded people, and having flying lessons every day, we were both hooked and joined the club the following year in March 1970.

During the holiday we had learnt, how to pilot a glider, how to act as ground crew, retrieve aircraft, carry out daily inspections and pre-flight checks, as well as how to attach a launch cable, act as signal man and control a launch safely. All instructions you wouldn't get paying for powered lessons.

Strapping in for a launch in a Slingsby T21

Open cockpit Slingsby T21 preparing for luanch

Our instructor on the course was an ex-RAF pilot, shown above with me in the club's Slingsby T21.

The other glider (Sailplane) we flew was a Slingsby T49 show below with Alan. This Sailplane had a canopy which kept you protected from the elements and we all preferred for that reason.

Alan standing beside the Slingsby T49 with the clubhouse and main hanger in the backround, July 1969

One of the second-hand dealers friendly with my dad, and whom I had met several times, was Larry Bleaken, a gliding instructor at the "Cotswold Gliding Club" based at Aston Down Airfield near Minchinhampton, and he suggested that we join there.

Nympsfield was primarily a ridge soaring site with a winch launch that would get you up to about 800 or 900 feet, whereas Aston Down was a RAF base with a long tarmac runway. They towed the gliders up using a tow-car, and a good launch could reach 1600 or 1700 hundred feet. You'd need to pay for an aerotow to get that sort of height at Nympsfield, and being a much bigger field, cable breaks on launch were far less hazardous.

The most hazardous thing that happens on a fairly regular basis when gliding is a cable breaking, which is why instructors spend so much time getting pilots used to it happening unexpectedly. Nympsfield was a short narrow field and options were limited if a cable broke. Sometimes you could be too high to simply put the nose down and land on, but not high enough to turn and complete a circuit.

Alan and I both took his advice and joined Cotswold Gliding Club in June 1970, but Alan left after the first year to pursue other interests. I stayed on, forming a friendship with "Andy" a flight controller on HMS Ark Royal, and whose parents ran the Weighbridge Inn at Longfords, the club's watering hole. Andy and I both went solo for the first time on the same day and celebrated by purchasing Champagne for everyone at the pub that night, as was the tradition.

Preparing for my first solo flight

I mentioned to Andy that a friend of mine, John Bryant, also served on the Ark Royal and asked if he knew him? I never got to the bottom of what had happened between them, but Andy's full answer is unprintable other than, "Yes I know the B******!"

I didn't enquire any further.

After going solo my weekends were nearly all taken up with gliding. The social life at the club was very good, with a lot of members of my age, and there were a number of parties.

On one occasion I was invited to a party that was going to be attended by a few members, and those of us, like me, who didn't live locally were told that we could stay over at a flat belonging to Cliff and his partner Sue, in Stroud.

Cliff was a local police Constable in Stroud and Sue was a nurse. On the day of the party, Cliff was working nights, so Sue drove Andy and I to the party in his car. Sue had rather a lot to drink at the party, as did another girl whose name I can't remember, but was a civilian colleague of Cliff's, and that Andy was hoping to make his girfriend. It was decided that Andy would drive her car back to the flat, and I would drive Sue home in Cliff's car.

I had no idea where Sue and Cliff's flat was so I had to follow Andy. Just as we pulled up outside the house in Stroud, I was suddenly aware of blue flashing lights behind me and a panda car pulled up, out of which stepped a very angry-looking police officer who I soon recognised as Cliff.

"Do you realise that you have just driven over half a mile, in my car! with a flat tyre?" he demanded, pointing to the rear offside wheel. At the same time he spotted his intoxicated girlfriend, asleep on the back seat and oblivious to the world. "What the hell is going on here?" he shouted, trying to think if there was anything he could arrest me for.

Trying to explain to an infuriated police officer, just how I came to be driving his car with a flat tyre and why his girlfriend was drunk on the back seat, was not the easiest thing I'd ever been called on to do.

After some explanation, backed up by Andy, and the now semi-conscious Sue, we were informed that Cliff's shift finished at 7:00 a.m. and that if he arrived home in the morning to find that his wheel had not been changed for the spare and the cost of a new tyre not been supplied, we would be very sorry. We certainly believed him, and not wanting to find out exactly what he had in mind, we set our alarm for six a.m.

As it turned out, Cliff phoned in the morning to let Sue know that it had been an interesting night all round, and that he wouldn't be home until he had completed mounds of paperwork. Heaving a sigh of relief, we took the car to a garage and had the tyre, which turned out to be quite worn, replaced with a re-tread.

Sue remained her old chatty, friendly self towards me at the club, but Cliff was never quite as friendly after that night.

When you first go solo and get your gliding certificate, you still have a check flight each time with an instructor before you go up alone, to make sure you're able to cope with the weather conditions of the day. On one such occasion, when I had Larry Bleaken in the back as P2, I found a thermal just waiting for me at the top of the launch. Larry decided he would let me get in some soaring practice rather than just do a circuit. Soaring involved locating the centre of any thermal you found and required practice. It turned out to be the longest and most memorable flight I ever had.

Larry was a very experienced instructor, but had a reputation as a bit of an eccentric and on this occasion he was in relaxed mode and decided to rest his feet on my shoulders, rather than the pedals. How he managed it I'm not sure. We had been in the air for about twenty minutes, when Larry announced that he was a bit concerned about how far we were from the airfield considering our height, and suggested that we start heading back. I turned the aircraft as instructed and headed towards the airfield. After a couple of minutes, Larry once again voiced his concern and told me to start heading back.

"I am heading back," I told him.

At which point his feet disappeared from my shoulders and he sat forward, he then pointed over my shoulder at the airfield in front of us, and said with some authority, "That's Kemble! ... Aston Down's over there." He pointed to our right before saying, "My aircraft," and taking over as P1. We did make it

Larry Bleaken (foreground)

back to the airfield, using all of Larry's skill as a pilot, but only just. It was a good thing the airfield was quite large because we had to land a bit short, forgoing the luxury of a normal approach. The retrieval team had a longer walk than usual to reach us and were not best pleased.

My logbook remarks column entry for that flight reads, "Good thermaling. Must watch rate of sink etc. and be prepared to turn in early if necessary. Need for good approach height clearly demonstrated. L. Bleakin C.F.I."

I should point out that at this time, in the late sixties and early seventies, Aston Down, although only used by the RAF as a storage facility, was a standby airfield for the Red Arrows Display Team, who were based at Kemble. The two airfields had looked very similar to me from the air, because on that day. as chance would have it, there were cars parked at the end of both runways. We used an old bus as a control tower, and it never occurred to me that there was no double decker bus to be seen where I was heading. Anyway, we both lived to tell the tale, and a valuable lesson was learned

As Aston Down was a standby airfield for the Red Arrows, we were always grounded if they were in the air. At the end of each day, we would have to form a line across the width of the runway, and walk its length looking for any stones, even quite small ones, that could pose a risk to any jet aircraft landing.

I remember on one occasion, a message came to us from the security gate that the Red Arrows were returning unexpectedly to Kemble from an airshow for some reason, and that we were to stop all flights until further notice. It was easy enough to stop launching aircraft, but one of our instructors, who owned his own sailplane, was already in the air, and we had no way of contacting him.

We notified Kemble tower, who warned the returning display team that there was a glider in the air, and that the pilot was unaware of their return. We waited to be given the all-clear to start flying again, and kept an eye out for our instrutor. It was probably no more than twenty minutes before we saw the spectacular sight of the Red Arrows fly overhead in formation, and on approach, heading for home.

Not long after, our instructor landed, and when he and the retrieval team returned to the bus, he put his head in and declared to everyone excitedly, "Bloody Hell! You'll never believe what just happened......I was doing a tight turn and the bloody Red Arrows went by in formation......right underneath me!"

Because the Red Arrows had been made aware of his presence and would have seen him, we think they must have decided that as he was so far above their flightpath, there was no reason to alter course. To hear our instructor tell it however, they were so close he thought he was going to join their formation! Anyway, it was the main topic of conversation in The Weighbridge that night.

View of Aston Down airfield from the air

Chapter 8

The Hall and Rohan Years

My father had worked hard securing a place for me with Hall and Rohan, with whom he had many dealings and a good relationship, so it would have been very hard not to accept it, especially as I had no real idea what else to do on leaving school.

Hall and Rohan was a well-established business trading from 'The Mall Galleries' 20 The Mall, Clifton, Bristol, from 1948. The Rohan in the name was the son of the dealer Thomas Rohan, of Bournemouth, who apparently was the author of several books about antiques.

Tony Hall was the sole proprietor when I joined in 1964, and was I believe a former Commando, who had been taken prisoner after being injured in action during World War Two. He was effectively running three separate businesses. An antique dealership, an antique restoration workshop, and a theatre hire company. The theatre hire side of the business meant that they had a large stock of antiques of all sorts, that were loaned out to various clients such as The Bristol Old Vic and the BBC.

These items would often come back from their tour of duty needing some repair, and the new apprentice, namely me, could be let loose, knowing that if I did mess up, I wasn't working on a piece that belonged to a valued client or was of national importance.

Hall & Rohan 20 The Mall Clifton

I joined the firm when the restoration workshop was still located on the first floor of number twenty, The Mall, but there was more to the property than just that over the shop. The first floor extended over the properties next door on both sides. The layout was a confusing maze of storage rooms and private flats, one of which was occupied by Mr Creasey, who was Tony Hall's second in command, and pretty much ran the restoration side of things, together with the theatre hire business.

Once I had started work, I really enjoyed what I was doing, as well as the unusual environment I found myself in. I was to serve my time as an apprentice under two men, Brian Riggs, who it turned out was a semi-professional magician of some note, and Carlo Perona, an Italian from San Remo in Northern Italy. It turned out the Brian much preferred to be called by his stage name "Mike Donnelli," and he was always introduced and known to friends and family as Mike. Mike and Carlo had an established daily and weekly routine that they quickly adapted to incorporate me.

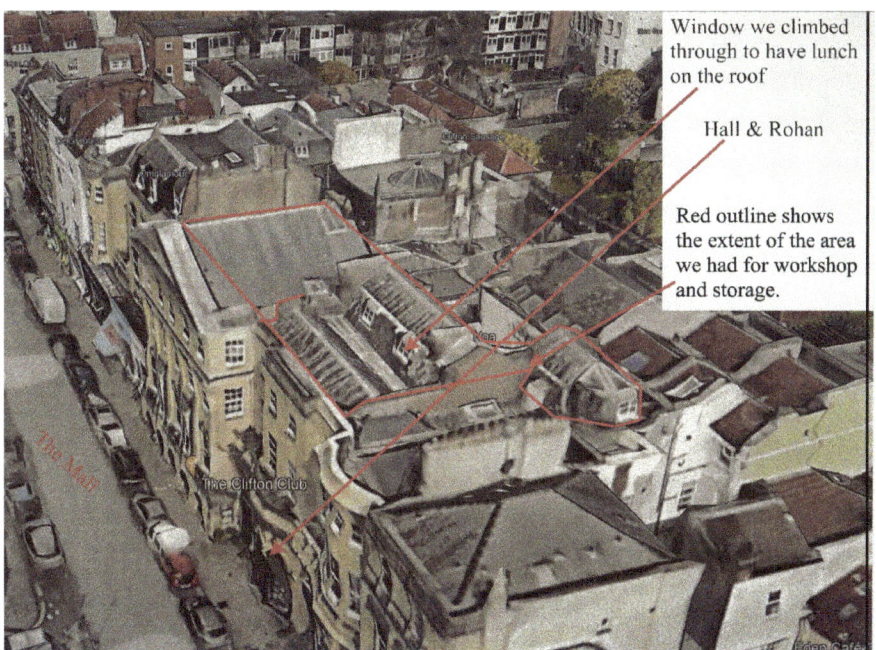

Upper floor of number 20 was a labyrinth

Mid-morning each day I was dispatched off to purchase cakes for our morning coffee break along with the latest copy of the Corriere della Sera newpaper for Carlo from Smith's, and any cigarettes or tabacco they needed. Lunch was normally eaten in the workshop, unless it was a warm day, when we would often climb out of an upper window and partake of a picnic on the roof. Monday was the one exception, when rain or shine, summer or winter, we would drive to a transport cafe on Cheltenham Road. Why that particular cafe I never found out.

Brian (Mike) on the left and Carlo on the right, having lunch outside a country house where we set up a workshop to restore the furniture on site, 1964

Other traditions that were alway adhered to were finishing early on Christmas Eve, when Mr Creasey would deliver our wage packet for the week, which would include a Christmas bonus, and Carlo would supply a bottle of Cinzano, and some cheese and crackers would appear from somewhere, so we would all have a drink together, before starting the Christmas holiday.

The other tradition was the firm's Christmas Party. This took place on the last Friday before Christmas and was attended by all the staff plus Mrs Creasey, Derek Cornwall, another dealer with a shop in the Mall, and any spouses who wished to attend, normally a dozen or so people. Several bottles of expensive champagne would be opened, to be consumed with the traditional crackers and cheese. There would be a couple of toasts, and then Mike would perform some close up magic to entertain everyone, a role that I would later take on after Mike left the firm.

Carlo spoke in his very own style of broken English that took some time to get used to, but when you did, you discovered that he also had a unique sense of humour. Something I discovered during my second week in the job.

I had been given the task of cleaning the florescent lights that illuminated the main workshop. They were fairly ordinary long tubes but they had a thin metal industrial style shade that ran the length of the tube and stuck out from either side by a good six inches.

A thick layer of sawdust had collected on top of the shades and Mike, had dispatched me up a set of steps with a dust pan and brush to clear it off before he started repolishing a cabinet.

When Carlo came into the room he asked me what I was doing, and I told him.

After a moment's thought, he beckoned me down the steps saying, "No, dees no good, you no clean same dees...eh takea too long eh? Carlo, e show you quick way for clean eh."

Taking me by the arm he led me over to some shelves where there were various spray tins of gold paint that had been used on some project for the Bristol Old Vic. He selected a tin that he determined by shaking was just about empty, before spraying what little paint remained into a cardboard box. He then walked me over to the gas ring that we used for heating the glue pot and proceeded to light the gas, rest the spray tin on the gas-ring and then ushered Mike, who had been oblivious to proceedings thus far, and I, out of the room.

The three of us stood outside the door waiting until there was a loud "BANG" from inside. Mike was a little surprised, as he still had no idea what had happened, but was obviously used to Carlo's antics.

As we re-entered the room it was as if it was raining sawdust. The shockwave from the explosion having displaced much of what had been on the shades.

Carlo pointed to the sawdust rain and declared triumphantly, "Dah, you see....now isa clean ah...I tell you isa quick way...no?"

I had expected some sort of reaction, even anger from Mike, but he simply returned to whatever it was he had been doing before, obviously not surprised in the least by what had just occurred, but did point out to Carlo that he wanted the room dust free for polishing.

This was the first of Carlo's crazy antics that I witnessed during my time at Hall and Rohan, but it was by no means the last. Carlo did make amends by sprinkling water around the floor before helping me to sweep up

Brian Riggs, (Mike Donnelli) was a gifted restorer by day and a talented magician on the weekends, and he introduced me to the world of magic and cabaret entertainment.

I had always loved watching magicians such as David Berglas and David Nixon on the television, and Mike could see how interested I was in learning some effects. He soon taught me some illusions and introduced me to the Bristol Society of Magic.

Somtimes Mike would take me along to help him set up, and start the tape recorder for his music if there was no band to play for him. He had an assistant who would sometimes be part of the act, but it depended on the venue and whether or not she was available.

Mike Donnelle performing his Cabaret act

I became an active member of the Bristol Society for several years, being asked to perform at many of their events, including their annual show at the Y.M.C.A. theatre in 1967.

It was novel and exciting at the time to see my name on posters.

I also became more proficient at sleight-of-hand, and won the Society's Close-up competition in 1966.

Performing sleight-of-hand and close-up magic for small groups of guests at hotels and functions was a very different skill to performing cabaret, but I had good tutors at the Society.

At one of the magic society's open days, I performed my cabaret act in front of our Honourary Presedent, His Honour E. H. C. Wethered, O.B.E. M.I. M. C., and as a result of that, I was asked to do the act at the Y.M.C.A. Theatre for a second time in 1969.

I had by this time put together a Cabaret Act and wanted to follow in the footsteps of Mike Donnelli and start performing professionally. This meant that I had to get an agent, and Mike gave me the name of his.

Poster advertising the Y.M.C.A. show 1969

However Mike was a well established entertainer with a tour of London's West End on his C.V. and his agent was not one to take on untried acts.

However I did receive the following letter, and after performing in front of a night club audience for the first time, I was accepted onto the books of Len May.

LEN MAY ENTERTAINMENT DIRECTION
Licensed by the City and Council of Bristol
(Member of the Agents Association Ltd.)

Managing Director:
Len May
Secretary:
Margaret J May

46 Falmouth Road, Bishopston, Bristol 7 Tel. 47905

Cabaret, Concerts, Variety and General entertainment agency. Contractors for Star Radio And Television Artistes.

8th. October, 1966.

Dear Sir,

Your letter to Mr. Len Thomas has been passed on to us, we would be interested in seeing your act, and if you are free on Saturday, 15th. October, and would care to do your act at Mardon's Club, Trinity Street, Bristol. 1. Before a live audience, we may then be able to offer you some bookings.
Mardon's Club is between the Royal Hotel and the Cathedral, College Green, the show starts at 8-0. p.m.

Yours faithfully,

Len May

Copy of the letter I received from Len May asking to see my act

Len May procured me bookings, firstly at British Legion and working men's clubs, but then later, after he saw that my act was becoming more sophisticated and polished, at night clubs and hotels.

To receive bookings from Len May, I had to perform two twenty minute spots. The stage act that I performed at the Little Theatre was a manipulation act to music that constituted my first spot. My second spot was a conventional patter act, incorporating, some card tricks, and some mind reading with jokes and humour thrown in.

Being a bona fide entertainer entitled me to join the Greenroom Club that was situated in Colston Street, where many of the other local entertainers would have a drink or a late-night meal. It was also a convenient place for visiting performers who were in plays or shows at the Hippodrome to relax. I joined not so much because I thought I would use it much, but more, I confess, in order to show off the membership card to my friends. It made me feel like a bit of a celebrity, the vanity of youth I suppose. On the other hand I think all entertainers, just want to show off.

Performing at a nightclub Christmas 1970

The 1960s was a good time for nightclubs and there were some places where you could have a drink, a decent meal, a gamble on the roulette or blackjack tables and at the same time enjoy a cabaret show. The usual format for a cabaret show at a nightclub would be a Vocalist or Musician, a Comedian and a speciality act, either a Juggler, an Acrobat or Magician, often followed by an Exotic Dancer (Stripper).

Unfortunately, legislation was passed in the late sixties preventing gambling licences being granted to premises that had other activity (entertainment) under the same roof. The thinking behind it being that cabaret and drinking were social activities, and that encouraging gambling was inappropriate in that environment. The unwanted side effect was that many of the clubs became less profitable and closed down.

Of course, when I first started work at fifteen, I had to cycle to and from Clifton, but as soon as I turned sixteen, I applied for a provisional driving licence and bought a motorbike. I say motorbike, but it was hardly that, it was a B.S.A. Dandy, a sort of moped without the pedals. However, I found it very difficult to get on with the unconventional pre-select gears.

B.S.A. Dandy

Unlike the Vespas and Lambrettas of the time, which required you to pull in the clutch lever, select the gear you wanted and then release the clutch, with the Dandy you had to select the gear you wanted first, and only then pull in and release the clutch.

I soon replaced the Dandy with a more conventional scooter, an Agrati Capri, that I bought second-hand from a bike shop in Cotham Hill. I didn't keep it very long, partly because of the pre-select gear thing, and partly because I felt a bit inferior if I went anywhere with my friend Chris, who had a "proper" motorbike, as well as a cool looking crash helmet, or skid-lid, as he insisted on calling it.

Me with my Scooter trying to look cool

This was around the time when the news was often reporting on pitched battles between Mods and Rockers at sea-side resorts like Weston-super-Mare.

For those of you who are too young to remember, the Mods and Rockers were two distinct youth cultures of the early to mid-1960s.

The Rocker culture was centred around motorcycling, and their dress reflected that, with Rockers wearing protective clothing such as black leather jackets and motorcycle boots, although they sometimes wore a type of thick soled plimsole, known as "brothel creepers" instead, like the earlier Teddy Boys, although their style was heavily influenced by Marlon Brando in the film "The Wild Ones."

The common Rocker hairstyle was a pompadour, while their music genre of choice was 1950s rock and roll, played by artists including Eddie Cochran, Gene Vincent and Bo Diddley.

A sixties Rocker with his bike

The Mod culture was centred on fashion and music, and many Mods rode scooters that were customised by adding large numbers of rear-view mirrors and spot lights.

Mods wore suits and other clean-cut outfits, but would often don ex-military parkas whilst riding their scooters.

They listened to 1960s music genres such as soul, rhythm and blues, ska, beat music, and British blues-rooted bands like The Yardbirds, The Small Faces and The Who. "

I think I must have thought about both the expense and wind resistance of fitting too much chrome, and ended up with just two mirrors. Not so much as a fashion statement, more to be able to see what was behind me.

Driving to and from work on a scooter made me feel much more adult, and I thought gave me a much better chance of chatting to a girl I had spotted working in the hairdressers further up The Mall, and asking her on a date.

I had recognised her as a girl who had been in a different class to me, but the same year at secondary school.

The girl in question, Pauline, remembered me when I approached her and we did meet for lunch on The Downs a couple of times, but she soon moved on to another hair salon in town and we lost touch.

A typical 1960s Mod

One of the first places I was shown after starting work at Hall & Rohan was the Merchant's Hall on the Promenade, a wide and impressive thoroughfare that runs up into Clifton Village from the top of Bridge Valley Road. It is also the address of The Mansion House and Engineer's House, and other properties where we carried out work.

Merchant's Hall home of the Society of Merchant Venturers

We seemed to be forever repairing the same chairs from The Merchant's Hall, and I can remember Carlo commenting to Mr Creasey about it one day, asking why it was that we often had to repair the same chairs over and over again. He wanted to know if there were some particularly large people using the chairs and breaking them.

We were both astonished when Mr Creasey informed Carlo that they were not in fact the same chairs, but different dining chairs from the same set.

Carlo uttered his usual exclamation in Italian, "Porco Dio," (*apologies to any Italians reading this*), "how many chair e av in dis set ?"

To which Mr Creasey's reply was "Ninety"

Not only that we were told, "They have a table they can fit them around for banquets!"

It turned out that, as the number of members increased, so more chairs were made for the set and more sections were made to extend the table for official banquets.

Just some of the Chairs we repaired over the years

When I was taken to visit the Merchant's Hall, it was just after Tony Hall had managed to find a piece of very rare Bristol hard paste porcelain, a single tea cup that I was told was worth a great deal of money.

Bristol was one of the first places in Britain, along with Plymouth and New Hall in Staffordshire, to make true porcelain.

Three pieces of Bristol hard paste porcelain

Of course, one room in Merchants Hall boasted a display cabinet full of Bristol porcelain, including a complete dinner service, and several large centre pieces. One of the other treasures I was shown during that memorable visit was the saddle that Queen Elizabeth the First had used on her visit to Bristol in 1574. It was housed in a hermetically sealed cabinet set in the wall. Since that time however, I have been in communication with Merchant's Hall and I have been informed that the saddle has been reassessed, and is now believed to date from the early 18th century. So not Elizabethan, but still a very rare item and in excellent condition.

Another location I remember being given a guided tour of was The Red Lodge. The Red Lodge Museum is a historic house and museum in Park Row. The original building was

Tudor/Elizabethan, and construction began in 1579. The main additional building phases date from the 1730s and the early 19th century. Because I had lived for many years on St Michael's Hill I was very well aquainted with the strange little red door, and had walked past it many times on various missions into town. I knew nothing about the building that lay behind it however, other than it was called the Red Lodge.

The Red Lodge with the controvertial sign removed

At the back of the property is the knot garden, a walled garden that recreates one of the gardens of the Lodge as it might have been 400 years ago, being designed around low box hedges, knotted together on a gravel base taken from a pattern in the plasterwork of the house's bedroom ceiling. Small gardens of this type were known as "closed knots." Other gardens, known as "open knots" were simpler but more extensive, and were always enclosed by a perimeter hedge and sometimes resembled parterres. Most of the plants used in the knot garden would have been common in the Elizabethan period.

When the building in Park Row came on the market in 1919, it was purchased to create a headquarters for the "Tribe," as the collective membership is known, of the "Bristol Savages," a group of local artists who would meet regularly to sketch and paint together in their "Wigwam. Annual exhibitions have continued since that date, apart from a break during World War II. Past members include etcher Stanley Anderson, painter William Titcomb and sculptor Frank Dobson.

The former Bristol Savages logo

Unfortunately, in recent years, the Bristol Savages have been accused of racism and cultural appropriation because of their name and logo, which features the stylised head of a Native American man wearing a war bonnet, They also meet in what they call the Wigwam and refer to themselves as the Tribe. In 2020 they gave in to pressure and the name was changed to "Bristol 1904 Arts".

I have mentioned already that Hall and Rohan had a thriving theatre hire business and there was an occasion when some of our older-looking tools were loaned out to the BBC for one of their productions. I can remember being taken to the studio to see them setting up an old shipwright's workshop on set, ready for filming. I didn't really appreciate then, how lucky I was to be given access to all these places.

The day eventually came when we moved out of number twenty. The shop moved up The Mall to numbers 36 and 38, and the workshop moved into large premises in Waterloo Street.

This property had a large main workshop, a machine-shop, a polishing-shop and several storage rooms.

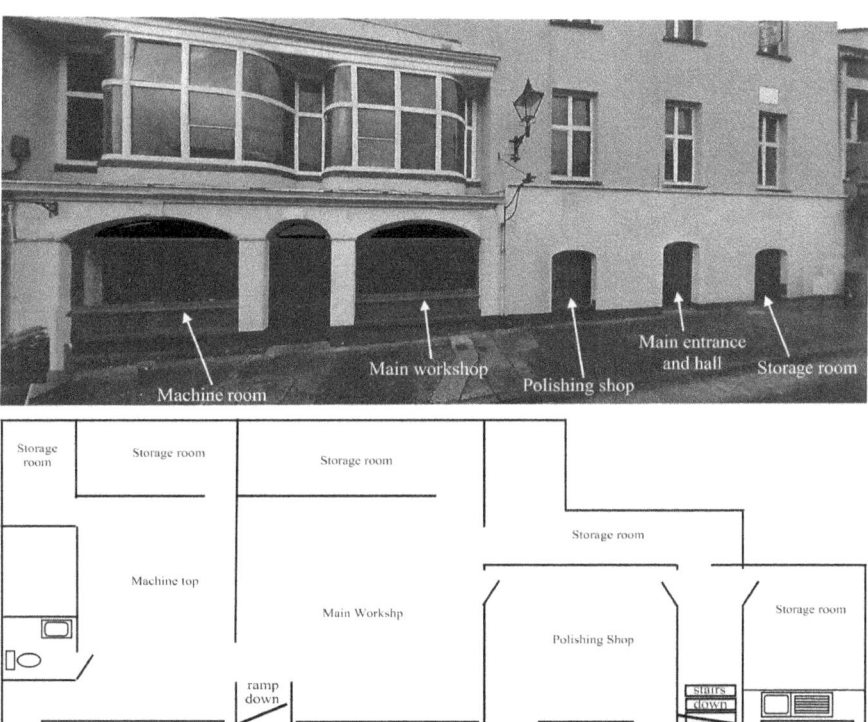

Workshop in Waterloo Street

The firm had a solid fuel central heating system installed before we moved in with the solid fuel boiler in the main workshop.

Mike, Carlo and myself had the task of moving everything from the existing workshop in The Mall to the new workshop in Waterloo Street, a job that took us several days.

Another example of Carlo's sometimes reckless behaviour was the fact that we found three rounds of live rifle ammunition stood up on an internal shelf, and some discussion took place as to what we should do with them.

However, Carlo calmly picked them up and dropped them in the solid fuel stove.

Mike and I stood well back apprehensively until we heard three rather disappointing "Phuds" and Carlo simply announced, "Is OK now, Carlo... e dispose...eh."

I should explain that Carlo's family lived in San Remo just over the border from the French Riviera, and during the war Carlo served in the Italian Navy, so he, like many others of his generation, were no strangers to explosives. He once told me how he used to go fishing by throwing hand-grenades into a lake and picking up stunned fish when they floated to the surface. It explained a great deal.

Whereas my father had been reluctant to talk about the war, Carlo would tell me about many of his experiences. How many were exaggerated, and to what extent I don't know. Many involved his time on leave in San Remo, when the Germany Army was pulling out.

His family ran a small hotel and his mother and sister had been on friendly terms with a couple of German officers who used to drink in the bar. On the last night before the German army was to leave they came knocking on the door late at night and in some distress. They feared that they would be sent to fight in Russia, and were intending to desert.

They asked if Carlo's family would hide them, and if so they would return in the morning early. Carlo's family insisted that it they were to risk hiding them, they would have to be hidden there and then, that it would be too dangerous in the morning. The officers insisted that they had to do something first and would return as soon as possible, Carlo said that they should have taken his advice; his family never saw the officers again.

One of the things we used to do to save money, was to solder to length and repair our own bandsaw blades, rather than pay a firm to do it. To this end we made a jig to hold the tapered ends of the blade in place while they were soldered with silver solder. The necessary heat was supplied through a welding gun connected to both the mains gas, (coal gas at that time) and a pair of large foot operated bellows.

The sequence of events was as follows. The prepared ends of the blade, together with flux and an amount of solder were first clamped in the jig, then Carlo would turn on and light the gas and I would operate the bellows. One day I told Carlo that we had at home an old cylinder vacuum cleaner that you could set to blow instead suck, simply by attaching the hose to the other end of the cylinder. You could possibly use that instead of the bellows, I suggested.

Carlo thought it was a good idea, so from that time on it only needed one man. Carlo would light the gas, turn on the vacuum cleaner and adjust the amount of airflow with the air tap on the blowgun.

This all worked extremely well until the fateful day Carlo's lighter failed to work. Either it was out of fuel or needed a new flint. Anyway, realising that he needed matches he called over to me to find a box. Whilst waiting for me to locate matches Carlo turned off the gas tap on the blowtorch, but not the main gas tap on the wall, not realising that gas, although not escaping from the blowtorch, was instead going back down the airline and filling up the cylinder vacuum cleaner.

It had taken me a while to locate the much-needed matches, but when Carlo eventually turned on the gas tap on the blowtorch and lit the gas, nothing seemed other than normal.

However, unbeknown to us, the vacuum cleaner was by then full of gas, and the resulting "BANG!" when it was switched on, together with the very impressive sheets of flame that emerged from both ends of the cylinder, was one of the scariest things I have ever witnessed.

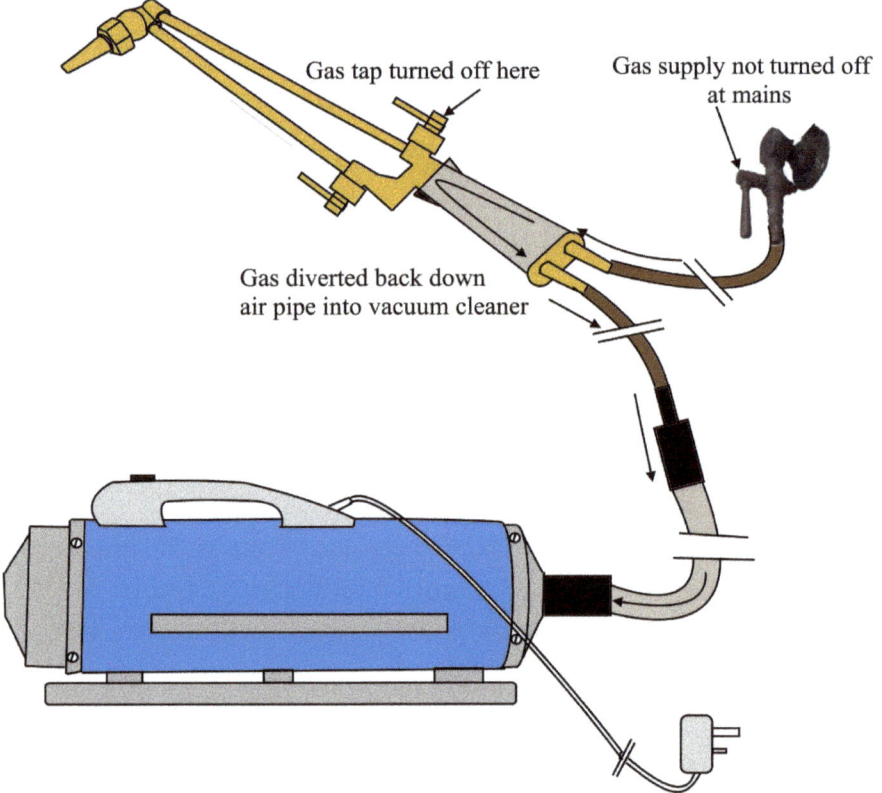

We didn't realise that the gas was being re-routed bown the airline into the vacuum cleaner's cylinder

Even Carlo jumped and uttered his familiar expletive "Porco Dio!" This, along with "Porca Madonna" and the very bad

"Vaffanculo!" were among the first Italian words I became familiar with. (I apologies once again to any Italian readers for the language.)

It's a fact that during the nine years I worked with Carlo, his English improved some, but my command of the English language deteriorated considerably. However, I have to say that I learnt a huge amount about, life and philosophy, as well as furniture restoration from Carlo.

There were also some joyously funny moments we shared. Carlo and I had got into a routine whereby, around 10am we would take a walk to Smiths to get his daily paper, the Corriere della Sera, and we would purchase a cake in the bakers on the way back.

Carlo taight we a grear deal more than just Furniture restoration

This meant that we crossed Regent Street into Princess Victoria Street on the way back to the workshop. On one occasion Princess Victoria Street was blocked by a delivery van that had double parked outside, but on the opposite side of the road to the bakery, blocking the road. Whoever had been driving the car directly behind the van, realising he would be held up for some time, had taken the opportunity to pop into one of the other shops to make a quick purchase, leaving his car unattended.

Carlo and I had crossed the road between the delivery van and the now unattended car to enter the bakery, and as Carlo was ordering our cakes, an extremely angry chap stormed into the bakery and pointing out into the street, demanded of Carlo, that he move his car.

Looking out of the window it was immediately obvious to Carlo what had happened. The delivery van had moved off, meaning that it was now the driverless car that was holding up the traffic. This irate chap had obviously turned into the road just in time to see Carlo and I crossing in front of the car and falsely assumed that Carlo was the driver of the car blocking the road.

Carlo, in true Carlo fashion, decided to milk the situation as much as possible and turned to the man and raised his hands palms out, as if signaling the rider of a horse to halt, and calmly said, "Skusee, Una momenta please, I buya di cake me......you wait una moment...please"

The ensuing conversation between a somewhat amused Carlo and this very angry man continued something like this.

"Move your bloody car first...can't you see your blocking the road!!"

"Momenta...please, I buya di cake now...den we talka...eh."

Carlo paid for the cakes and then tuned to the man again, "Now....uh you want eh?"

"What I want is for you to move your bloody car you idiot, can't you see it's holding up all the traffic!"

In order to verify Carlo asked, pointing to the offending vehicle, "Sorry eh, you wanta Carlo to mova dis car?".

"Finally I'm getting through...yes"

"No" said Carlo with a shrug of his shoulders and a puzzled expression on his face...."Carlo, ...e no mova dis car ah"

"What do mean....you're not going to move it?"

"I no mova dis car" Carlo repeated, barely holding in a grin.

"What!...Why not?"

"Becausa.....Isa no my car dis one" Carlo explained.

It took a moment for Mr Angry to realise his mistake, but by that time the real owner of the car had finished his bit of shopping and had returned. As he drove away it was now the car of Carlo's angry assailant that was the cause of the hold-up. The expression on the man's face when he realised, was one of the funniest things I'd seen.

It was typical of Carlo, who I witnessed on several occasions pretend not to understand a question, in order to milk it. I remember when we had two fire extinguishers fitted to a wall in the workshop, one $Co2$ and one dry foam.

When Mr Creasy pointed to them, anxious that Carlo should understand which should be used on different fires, he asked Carlo, "What would you do if there was a big fire in the workshop Carlo?"

To which Carlo's reply was, "If isa big fire in da workshop!... I go home me!"

Mr Creasy looked at him slightly horrified, so Carlo explaind, "Carlo no stupid eh....if isa small fire, I taka da extinguisher, I try for put out da fire...But... ah you want?...if isa big fire...Carlo... e go home!"

On another occasion he came back from taking a test for his English driving licience, and said that the examiner had asked him several questions, mostly on the highway code, but also asked him what he would do if he had an accident on the road? He said that because of the examinerss expression, he wasn't sure if he had given an acceptable answer.

"What was your answer?" I asked.

Carlo told me he replied, "If I ava da accident...I lie still and I wait for de ambulance eh." but I'm not convinced this was his answer, I think it was just for my ears.

When Carlo purchased his Leyland Mini, it was at a time when cars were frequently being broken into and having their radios stolen. One company came up with the perfect solution. Carlo's radio was mounted under the front passenger glove shelf in a case. The idea was that the owner would insert a key into a slot at the side of the case and the radio could then be pulled out and taken away from the car. The radio could also have batteries inserted so that when out of the car, it could be used as any normal portable radio.

At that time, the shop and office could ring through to the workshop on an extension phone.

Mr Creasey would always ring the workshop first thing each morning, as well as several times throughout the day.

The phone, was located on a small desk and just to the right of it was a wall bracket on which stood a large valve radio set, that was constantly on. Whenever the phone rang, the first thing Mike would do was turn down the volume on the radio, so he could hear the call.

Mike was always the last to arrive in the mornings, and Carlo had hatched a plan. He had shown me his new car radio, and suggested that it was small enough to fit inside the large valve set near the phone. He removed the back of the set, tuned his car radio into the same station, and replaced the sets on the shelf.

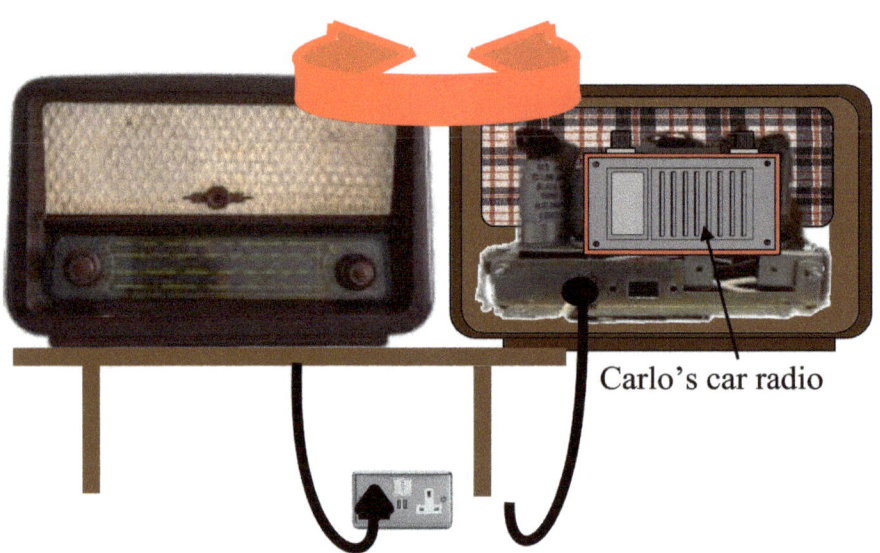

Carlo's car radio

We tuned both radios into the same station

That morning when the phone rang. Mike turned down the volume on the radio as usual. Puzzled by the fact that the volume remained unaltered, he turned the radio off and on several times.

We need to get a new radio, he told us, "The switch is broken on this one, I can't turn it off."

Carlo and I walked over to see what the problem was, as Mike answered the phone and and said he would ring back.

As we walked over Carlo suggested that the set could be possessed, and said he knew a priest he could call. In fact, the Catholic priest he referred to was a friend of Carlo, and would sometime pop in and try to persuade Carlo to attend his church.

By this time Mike had even unplugged the set from the wall, but still couldn't silence it!

We only just managed to stop Mike from picking the radio up and smashing it on the floor, along with Carlo's battery radio.

The words that came out of Mike's mouth when he knew what Carlo had done, would not have been suitable if Carlo had called a priest.

When I was seventeen, I started driving lessons with The British School of Motoring and managed to pass my driving test after 15 one hour lessons in a 1965 Triumph Herald.

The hunt was on for a car, and very foolishly, I decided it was more important to own a car than a collection of old weapons. The decision to sell my collection in order to obtain enough money to buy a decent car, was possibly the worst one I have ever made from a financial point of view. The value of the collection I had then, even if you discount the one or two firearms that would have had to be either deactivated or handed in to be destroyed, would have been in the tens of thousands, The original pepperbox that I purchased and sold for less than £20.00, would now retail at more than £3,000. If I sold the collection today I could buy at least a top of the range Jaguar, rather than a seven year old banger.

In the end, it was my father who found a suitable vehicle at Runway Motors Patchway, a car dealership on the A38 north of Bristol that was managed by one of his customers. The car was a 1959 Vauxhall Victor in lime green. (See page 165)

This was a lovely car, bench seat, column change and equipped with a built-in radio. All of a sudden, I was completely independent.

The following year I went on a touring holiday in the car, with Alan from next door, and Richard, Mr Hall's driver from work, with whom I had become friends. We spent a couple of weeks touring Wales, before crossing the Mersey Tunnel and heading back to Bristol on the M6 and M5 motorways, motorways still being a fairly new feature at the time.

Amongst friends and family I have acquired a reputation over the years of changing my cars as often as most people change shoes, but I have to disagree.

Hillman Imp same colour and model as mine

During the time I worked for Hall and Rohan I only owned four, the Vauxhall Victor that you have already been introduced to, a blue Hillman Imp, and a Blue Hillman Minx.

Carlo had by now bought a British Leyland Mini, and my friend Chris had likewise purchased a new Mini.

So obviously I couldn't be left out, and soon purchased my first brand new car.

A British Leyland Mini 850, YHU 969 J. Strange now to think that some of the optional extras that could purchased included a radio, footwell rubber mats and, believe or not, a heater! Total price including road tax and delivery came to around £617.00, on the road.

Eileen with YHU 969 J photographed in South Wales

My first car, the Vauxhall Victor was memorable for two reasons. Firstly because when driving back from London with Geoffrey Capstick in the passenger seat I experienced my first road traffic accident. We stopped at some temporary traffic lights, and the driver of the car behind only realised that the traffic had stopped when it was too late. He swung out to try and avoid a collision, but didn't quite manage it. The end result was that luckily nobody was injured, and after we had pulled the rear panel away from rubbing on the wheel the car was still driveable. The amazine thing was that, although it was the most prominent part of my car that had taken the impact, housing the turn indicator light, and was now much closer to the rear window than the designer had intended, the bulb was unbroken and the light still worked!

Secondly, because of the time I had Chris and his brother Stephen in the car, driving through the Lions of Longleat. The attraction had only opened in April of that year, and as it was the first drive through Safari Park outside Africa at the time, it was very busy. The signs told you to keep your car windows closed at all times and to keep moving. You were not supposed to stop the car to take photographs, or any other reason, and of course getting out of the car would have been very dangerous indeed.

On the day we were there, it was very busy and people were ignoring the rules about not stopping the car. It was just like a modern motorway tail-back. It was hot in the car with the windows closed, and to make matters worse, Chris announced that he was desperate for a pee.

Now I have to admit that neither Steve nor I were at all sympathetic to Chris's plight, and were constantly pointing out nearby trees that he could go behind.

"I don't see any lions near that one," we would comment, laughing, but I have to admit that when we did finally exit and locate a toilet block, Chris did look to be in some pain.

Before becoming interested in gliding, Chris and I had talked about having some scuba diving lessons. Although Chris was given a clean bill of health by his doctor, mine advised me that, because I'd always suffered with catarrh and bronchial problems, he thought it could be a potentially dangerous activity for me to take up.

Chris did become heavily involved in diving however, and went on to become a diving instructor. This didn't prevent me from being able to persuade him to come to Nympsfield on a few occasions, and he sometimes invited me to join him snorkel diving around St. Catherine's Island off Tenby, sometimes with his brother Stephen, who had also been a friend and classmate of mine at Bishop Road, but who left to attend police college,

St Catherine's is an interesting tidal island, and for many centuries a tiny church was the only building on it, but the construction of St Catherine's Fort in 1867 necessitated the demolishing of the remains of the church.

St Catherine's Island

The island was operated as a zoo from 1968 to 1979, which was run by the Batt family, relatives of Chris and Steve. The family I remember, had a pet mongoose, which would greet new visitors like myself by running up to them and urinating on their shoes. They had no guest room, so on the odd occasion Chris and I stayed over, we took sleeping bags, and stayed in a room at the top of the fort on makeshift beds that we assembled from what chairs and benches we could find. I remember trying to get off to sleep on these make-do camp beds against the thunderous background noise of the tide, pounding in and out through the cave that ran from front to back of the island.

The island was just off the beach, and access to it on foot could only be made for a brief period at low tide. On one memorable occasion, the three of us had to change into our swiming trunks in the cramped confines of my Hillman Imp in the small harbour carpark, then help each other on with wet suits, and swim out to the island.

At low tide we walked back to get Chris and Steve's scuba gear, and I spent some time snorkel diving before returning to the island and basking in the sun, waiting to be joined by the would be Jacques Cousteaus. Like a fool, I managed to get very sun-burnt. On the drive home I started to feel decidedly unwell and the next day it was apparent that I had suffered mild sun-stroke and I was covered in burns from head to toe. The sunburn was so bad that I had to take a few days off work, being covered in huge blisters. For weeks after I recovered, I left a trail of dead skin behind me as the burns peeled.

As I mentioned, although Chris had taken up diving, he still visited the gliding club with me on a couple of occasions, just as I would go snorkelling with him at Tenby. However, it was not so much for the gliding, I think it was more because the couple who ran the Rose and Crown, Mr and Mrs Waymen, had two daughters, Jill, who I got to know when Alan and I stayed there on our gliding hoiday, and her sister who was a nurse at the B,R.I. where Chris was working as a porter.

Now I have always been what I consider to be a very careful driver, always keeping to a speed that I consider appropriate for the road conditions. Some other drivers, less careful than myself, interpret this as being a slow driver, something I dispute.

On one occasion, driving home from The Rose and Crown, in the dark, after a day's gliding, and with Chris in the car, (a blue Hillman Minx as I remember) Chris decided to make a sarcastic reference to the speed I was doing.

"What happens when you put your foot down?" he asked.

As it happened, we were on a reasonably straight stretch of road at the time, so I floored the accelerator pedal, expecting Chris to feel the sudden full thrust of the 1500cc engine. In fact, what happened was that the accelerator cable broke, the car slowed to a crawl and the engine revs shot through the roof. It took a minute or two for us to realise what had happened, turn off the engine, (no power steering back then) and coast into a convenient layby.

It was almost 11:00 pm and I wasn't a member of either the AA or the RAC. We talked for a while about what we were going to do, and after a little fiddling with the adjustment screws on the carburettor, we managed to adjust the tick-over sufficiently to start the engine again, put the car into second gear and drive off.

My Hillman Minx

A mile or so in second gear with only the tick-over determining the speed of travel got us to the junction with the A38, where luckily there was an all-night petrol station. The gods must have been in a good mood that night, because attached to the petrol station was a motorbike repair garage.

Our luck didn't extend to the garage having an accelerator cable for a Hillman Minx, but the proprietor of the garage was fortunately working late on a bike he was restoring. He also had a clutch cable for a motorbike, and after selling me the cable he was also kind enough to help feed it through from the carburettor, into the footwell of my car. What we couldn't do was attach the end of the cable to the accelerator pedal.

Both Chris and I are proud of the fact that we managed to cover the remaining 30 or so miles with us *both* driving. I was comfortable in the driving seat, steering and braking, and Chis was in a somewhat less comfortable position, half sitting and half crouching, while reaching into the footwell, grasping the end of the make shift accelerator cable.

After a few miles we became quite proficient. I would tell Chris when to increase or decrease the speed of our now dual control vehicle, and gear changes soon became second nature. I would simply warn Chris that a gear change was imminent by saying, "I'm going to change gear....now." At which time Chris would decelerate, I would select the required gear, and we would synchronise my letting up of the clutch, with Chris operating the accelerator cable.

When we arrived home, I had to admit that Chris had drawn the short straw, especially when he showed me his hands, which looked quite sore.

At home, life was looking good for the Holcombe family, with both sons in gainful employment and the family business doing well. However in late 1969, everything took a new turn, when my father had his first heart attack.

I had been out with friends, playing darts at The Bear and Rugged Staff behind Castle Park, and as usual had decided to finish off the night at Cleopatra's night-club in Easter

Compton. Returning home around 1.00am, I realised something was wrong as I approached the house.

Normally the place would have been in darkness at that time of night, with the rest of the family tucked up in bed, but the front-room light was on and the curtains of the corner window were drawn back. I knew something had happened straight away.

When I entered the front door and went upstairs, it became obvious that the intention had been for me to look in the front room, and when I did so I found a note from my brother telling me that they had called an ambulance for dad and that they were all at Southmead Hospital.

I rang the hospital and was told that a Mr Holcombe had been admitted with a suspected heart attack, so I waited, not sure what to do, without being able to contact my brother. There was always the chance I would pass them on their way back, if I chose to go to the hospital. It wasn't long however, before Ron and my mother returned and filled me in on just what had happened.

Dad remained in hospital for some days, and even when he returned home, he was confined to bed for some time.

Looking back, I can remember my father getting up in the night with what he assumed was very bad indigestion, but I wonder now whether it was in fact angina.

Dad had always been a chain smoker, lighting his next cigarette from the remains of his last one, and in a vain attempt to cut down, he started smoking cigars instead, not large ones like Churchill, but small Manikin cigars.

This reduced his smoking for a short time, but he was soon getting through several tins a day. In hospital after his heart attack the doctor told him in no uncertain terms that, it was his smoking that had caused his heart attack, and that if he didn't stop, there was nothing they could do for him.

Manikin cigar tin

The knowledge scared him so much, he never touched another cigar or cigarette for the rest of his life.

Being self-employed and therefore not receiving any sickness benefit, when dad was discharged he was advised to seek an easy job, one that didn't involve shifting heavy furniture or the stress of running a business. For several months he and mum lived off the property rents and savings alone, and dad decided to move to a property where he would't have to negotiate stairs.

At first, he decided that he would sell 6 Chandos Road and move into the house he owed in Bishop Road, but after the tenants had moved out, he determined it was too small and decided instead, to sell Bishop Road as well, and buy a house next door to The Spanish Guitar Centre in Elton Road.

4 Elton Road was a beautiful house, but dad soon became bored and converted the downstairs bedroom into an antique's showroom with access from the side alley. The side alley gave access to the back of the house and also a two-storey workshop that had previously been a graphic design studio, where the Babycham Logo had been designed.

Chapter 9

Self Employment

Back in the sixties there was no such thing as social media or online dating so if you wanted to meet members of the opposite sex, it was either at a dance, a friends party, work, a club, or, as my friend Alan and I decided, while attending a dance class. We therefore enrolled at the West of England Dancing Accademy in Clifton.

West of England Dance Accademy

A fancy name for a dance class run by one elderly tutor named Gladys Southgate, (no relation to my cousin Sylvia.)

Much like Waterloo, Trafalgar and the Tower of London however, it was to become the location where one of history's great events took place!.....No... I didn't learn to dance. But I did meet my future wife Eileen there, the best and luckiest thing that has ever hapened to me, I was soon informed.

Why this lovely young lady agreed to go out with me in the first place, let alone marry me, is still a mystery? Possibly she mistook me for someone wealthy, as she later claimed, I don't know? but if so, does that make me a victim of mistaken identity?

Whatever the truth of the matter, the history books record that we did in fact get married on the 9th September 1972 at Broadmead Baptist Church, and historians will no doubt debate the circumstances surrounding it for centuries.

Eileen and I before we became engaged

Once engaged, Eileen and I started to look for a house and get a mortgage.

In those days the building societies would only grant a mortgage over 25 years maximum, based on being able to make monthly repayments equal to no more than one week's net income. Despite Eileen being a nurse, which they classed as a profession, they would only take one third of her salary into account.

The Woolwich therefore granted us a twenty five year repayment mortage, that enableld us to purchase a terraced three bedroom house in Longfield Road St Andrew for £3,400.00, but not the corner property in Bishop Road that we preferred, that was on the market at £4,000.00.

I sold my British Leyland Mini to fund the deposit and purchased a cheap second-hand Mini as transport. Our monthly repayment was a manageble £20.00 per month! We had a year to do the house up before the wedding, so I had time to fit a kitchen, redo the bathroom and rewire the house.

I had been taught how to solder and wipe a lead joint in a water pipe by the time I was eight years old, as well as how to wire, not just an electric plug, but a lighting circuit, so designing, making and fitting a fitted kitchen was no problem.

I had been taught how to wallpaper a room professionally, as well as many other building skills. You could say I had started an apprenticeship as a plumber, an electricion, builder and glazier from the age of five. My father had also taught me to cut glass and upholster a squab seat before I started my second year of senior school, so I was never destined for an academic life, and probably couldn't have spelt it anyway.

I was shown how to do these things as I watched and helped my father with repairs, like the day we replaced a broken window in St Michael's Hill. I was shown how to cut glass and replace a pane, bedding it in with paint and putty. In the days before silicon sealant, if you wanted to make a joint water proof, you used pint and putty. Unfortunately, my knowledge of so many trades often caused friction when paying for some things to be done.

Our first house: 13 Longfield Road, with the blue second-hand mini that replaced my nice shiny new one. Even then a roof rack was considered a necessity

When we had a local builder replace a large slate roof on our house in Fishponds, for instance, it had a central gully that dropped down a step, and when I asked the builder if he was going to solder the joint in the zinc that seemed to me to be a potential souce of a leak in the future, he replied, "You can't solder an upright joint in zinc." Rather than stand on the roof and argue the point, I prepared some hydrocloric acid to use as a flux by disolving some pieces of zinc in it. Used a blow-lamp to heat one of my father's roofer's soldering irons, and soldered it myself over the weekend.

I never pointed it out to the builder in question, but he must have seen what I had done, and his attitude towards me after that was less than cordial.

Once my brother and I were both married, my father decided it would be a good idea to start a family business, by opening an antique shop. My brother and he would do the dealing and and run the shop, while I would run the restoration workshop.

Elton Road, was well suited for this purpose as it had a substantial two storey workshop at the rear.

My mini parked outside Elton Road where I was living when I met Eileen

Unfortunately it didn't work out, and I found employment working for Jones and Edwards, designing and making pine furniture in a workshop in Kingswood.

I designed a few pieces for them, including a corner dresser, and a tripod table. I also re-designed the dresser they had already been making, and made various other suggestions, some of which were taken on board and some not.

One of the first things I did was to re-design the dresser they were making, giving it a proper moulded plinth and large turned knobs for the drawers. Previously they had been fitting the same size knobs to both doors and drawers. and they were not easily convinced that two different sized knobs looked right.

In order to persuade them, I suggested that they put both versions of the dresser on display in their showroom next door, which they did.

Doug and I had just carried the new dresser into the showroom and placed it next

Standard Dresser with the larger drawer knob

to the old one on display, and were stood back comparing them, when a young lady came into the showroom, enquiring about the furniture we made.

Doug gave her a list of what we had to offer, and explained to her about the two dressers we were looking at, asking her whether she preferred the one with the large knobs on the drawers or the one with the same size knobs as on the doors.

Tripod Table

She looked at the two dressers and announced, "Oh...I much prefer the one with big knob!" before going a bright red from the neck up, turning away and walking out of the shop, never never to return.

Eileen and I became good friends with Doug Edwards and his wife Maureen, who ran "The Craft Pad," a gift shop on Gloucester Road selling hand made craft items, and also the furniture from the Kingswood workshop. We started going out for meals on a regular basis, and after I left and set up on my own, Doug and I would sometimes buy a piece of furniture or two as a joint venture, to restore and then sell in his shop.

When I started my own business, I built a lean-to workshop at the back of 13 Longfield Road, but in order to do so I had to lower the garden outside the back door by a good three feet. Harry Watts, who my father employed on many building projects and I alway knew as Unce Harry, gave me a hand. Between us, we loaded two large skips with earth by shovelling it into a wheel barrow, and taking it through what was the kitchen, through the dining room come new kitchen to be, along the passage, out of the front door, across the steps on a builder,s scaffolding plank to the front wall, and over another plank to the edge of the skip, where it came to a stop againts a block we had secured in place, where we lifted the handles and tipped the contents into the skip. I have no idea how many of these precarious journeys we made, but we did it. I must have been a great deal fitter that I thought.

Soon after I started in business, Eileen announced she was expecting our first child, Karen, who arrived two weeks late, and even then took her time about putting in an appaerance, but at least I was there to greet her.

Eileen with the newest member of the family at the back of 13 Longfield Road

At the time, if you wanted someone to repair your furniture and looked in Yellow Pages, there were plenty of upholsters and one or two French polishers listed, but only three antique furniture restorers. One I believe in Clevedon, another even further away, and Hall & Rohan in Clifton who stood out because they had a one eighth of a column entry. I decided to take the advice of the salesman at Yellow Pages and purchased a quarter column advertisement as shown.

Colin Holcombe
Antique Furniture Restoration

FREE ESTIMATES

For the
repair and restoration of
antique and fine furniture damaged
by central heating, wear, accident,
burglary, flood, fire, or
worm infestation

Telephone:
Bristol 33288

Advert in yellow pages

Once my business was set up, I was fortunate to be contacted by the curator of Harvey's wine museum in Denmark Street, and I was invited to quote for the restoration of the furniture in their recreation of an Elizabethan inn, "The Unicorn". Harvy's wine museum was located in the cellars below Denmark Street, and the Inn had been flooded.

Harvey & Sons Denmark Street

When I was young I can always remember people buying Harvey's cream sherry for presents, much like people give a bottle of wine now, although its difficult to find anyone who drinks sherry these days.

Every item of furniture in the musem passed through my workshop over the next three or four months and I had found an influential contact in Margaret Piggot, the curator.

It was from talking to Margaret, and having her show me the exhibits, that I began to learn something of the history of sherry production in Bristol, and it's sad to think that after hundreds of years of developing the brand and becoming synonymous with fine sherry, it's a thing of the past. Tastes have changed, and now because the EU have given legal regional status to the grapes that must be used, it is difficult to find any reference to Harvey's Bristol Cream.

Entrance to the Elizabethan Inn at Harvey's wine Museum

Harvey's wine-trading business was established in Denmark Street in Bristol in 1796. This was owned by William Perry, who went into partnership with Thomas Urch in 1822. Urch's nephew, John Harvey joined the firm as an apprentice, but by 1839, he was the senior partner in the Bristol branch of the family business and by 1871, the whole business was known as John Harvey & Sons.

In the late 17th century, sweetened Oloroso was hugely popular in the UK, and it was known as "*milk, sherry* or simply *Bristol Milk,*" because most of the sherry trade to the UK was passing through the port of Bristol at the time. Different types of wines arrived in Bristol and they were blended to create a sweet, smooth mixture.

One day in the 1860s, John Harvey II and his brother Edward were showing an aristocratic lady around their cellars, where she had some Harveys Bristol Milk. She was also asked to try a new, richer blend they had been working on, and she obviously enjoyed it, as she stated, *"If that is the Milk, then this must be Cream"* and so the new blend was named "**Bristol Cream,**" a brand trademarked since 1882.

At the start of the 1950s, Bristol Cream was the best-selling sherry in the world. It had been sold on such a massive scale that later the entire category of sweet/blended sherries was called Cream Sherry, and not the other way round as you may have thought.

From 1962, the business was known as Harveys of Bristol Ltd, and in 1966, the firm including all subsidiaries was bought out by Showerings Ltd. In 1960, the business relocated from Denmark Street to Whitchurch Lane, Hartcliffe and the Denmark Street cellars became Britain's only wine museum, with an adjoining restaurant. Both closed in 2003, but in 2016, the bar "Harveys Cellars" was located on the same site in Denmark Street.

In the 1990s, John Harvey & Sons began to sell Bristol Cream sherry in bottles made from Bristol blue glass, another product synonymous with Bristol.

Harvey's Bristol Cream was sold in Bristol Blue glass bottles

It's uncertain when Bristol blue glass was first made, but when the quality and beauty of the glass became known, it swiftly gained popularity, and as many as seventeen glass houses were set up in the city during the 18th century.

Bristol's glass makers were invited to demonstrate their skills at the Great Exhibition of 1851, but production ceased in about 1923, only to be revived again in 1988 and today is produced by The Original Bristol Blue Glass Ltd in Brislington.

With my business doing well and another addition to the family on the way, it was clear we needed to move. The ideal property presented itself in the form of 492 Fishponds Road, a large four bedroom corner house with a detached two storey workshop.

All should have been well if I had simply been able to take a week off and move, after all I had an eight month waiting list for work. Life is never that simple however.

The previous owners had gone bankrupt and were resentful that their home was being sold by the administrators to pay off their debts, and had obviously decided to make the move as difficult as possible.

492 Fishponds Road

The workshop had been used for storing fruit machines, and although it should have been cleared out on completion of the sale, it was still full. Although we could move in, I could not set up my workshop until some weeks later when it was finally cleared.

The cost of employing a removal firm to move us, on top of all the other expenses, seemed unnecessary, especially as we had good friends that could always be relied on. Chris Foulkes, as usual, was willing to help out with the actual move, (remember we were both young and fit back then), and Mike Letts gave us the use of his large van for the weekend.

Mike Letts, was a dealer I first met when his mother ran a second hand shop in The Mall called Treasure Trove. She was often doing deals with my father, and was also a close friend of Tony Hall. We became friends as well doing buiness together.

So on the 1st December 1976 with Eileen expecting our second child Susan, and now ordered not to do anything but rest after a visit to the maternity clinic, and having our two year old daughter Karen to look after, we moved into our new home.

The move was made more difficult by the fact that the building society had insisted the property was treated for woodworm. I had argued that I spent a lot of my time doing just that, but they insisted on contractors who would give a 25 year written guarantee.

The problem being that Chris and I had to move the furniture in while at the same time negotiating floorboards that had been taken up by the contractors. Add to that, the previous owners had taken, every lightbulb in the house, and most of the light fittings as well. To top it all off, they had removed the gas cooker, but instead of blocking the end of the pipe with a proper fitting, they left the end open and had simply turned off the gas inside the front door. Thank God we noticed before turning on the gas!

Our first night in the new property also turned into a nightmare. We had been unable to find Karen's cot so she came in with us. None of us could get to sleep because of the overpowering, and hazardous smell of the woodworm killer that had been sprayed under all the floors and throughout the loft. Concerned about us all breathing in potentially toxic fumes, we put on extra layers of clothing (remember it was December) and opened all the windows!

The next morning, we were roused by constant banging on the front door, and when I opened it, our next door neighbour, who soon became known as Mr Angry, was shouting in my face, demanding to know what the hell we were doing to create such a stink? and announcing that he was going to call in the environmental health people! So not a such bad start really.

My workshop in Alcove Road

While I was waiting for the previous owners to finally clear the workshop, I moved everything of theirs down to the ground floor, and started to prepare the upstairs to be my workshop. The biggest job was that the downstairs entrance was nothing more than the heavy sliding doors that you can see in the picture, and the upstairs consisted of barn doors that opened out. At some time in the past there had obviously been a pulley to lift or lower sacks. So a proper window upstairs and hinged doors downstairs were the first priority

When we lived in Longfield Road the young couple next door, Pauline and Steve had become good friends. Steve persueded me to play darts for The County Ground Hotel, and I became a regular team player on a Monday night. We then started playing Wednesdays for The True Blue Club at the Rovers ground, and occasionaly at Little Stoke Social Club on Fridays, when Pauline and Eileen would come along for home matches.

Steve was unemployed at the time of our move, so I agreed to pay him to help get the workshop ready. This was all costing me money at a time I wasn't earning, so I arranged for an overdraft allowance on my business account.

For a while business began to get back to normal until I had an accident in the Hillman Hunter Estate I owned at the time.

The accident was witnessed by two police officers in a patrol car that had been behind me, and prosecuted the other driver for driving without due care. Initially the insurance agreed to pay for the repairs and to the hire of a car whilst mine was in the garage.

This I did in order to continue in business, however hiring a vehicle was expensive and I was concerned at how long the repairs were taking. I rang the garage and was told that they were waiting for parts to be delivered. However, when the parts turned up and they started work, they discovered some rust in the floor, and the insurers decided that my vehicle was now a write-off. Now I was worried because the money they offered me was insufficient to get me back on the road with a decent estate.

The foreman at the garage suggested that they may continue with the repairs, if I paid for the repairs to the floor. which I agreed to. After a final wait for part to repair the floor, I was finally reunited with my car after 13 weeks.

However, not only had I been deducted a payment for what they referred to as betterment, because the replacement door and wing had replaced parts that had some rust. To rub salt into the wounds, they suggested that if I had accepted the write-off payment, I could have been back on the road within four weeks, and they would in that case only pay for four weeks car hire! This put me into debt with my bank, from which I never truly recovered.

I purchased a new car and I got a good deal from the Fiat showroom further up Fishponds Road with a Fiat Strada, to which of course I fitted a custom made roof rack as well as fitting a towbar for a trailer.

Fiat Strada with roof rack fitted

Business was ticking over, and I had some interesting work arrive, which involved making extra chairs to match existing sets. It was during this period that I began photographing some of my more intersting projects, some of which are recorded here

A bookmaker contact of Mike's, had purchased six Regency sable leg chairs that needed loose joints repaired and drop-in seats upholstered. He asked Mike if he could recommend someone who could not only do that, but maybe make two extra chairs to make a set of eight, and that to make any set complete it would be nice if the additional chairs were carvers.

Three become four

I had already made single chairs to match sets Mike had bought, so he recommended me. This however was a little different. It meant designing two arm chairs from scratch that would match the standards, and look as if they belonged. Carver chairs are larger overall, as well have having arms.

Set of six chairs with the two additional carvers

The five chairs I made into a set of six for Mike

This was certainly the work that I enjoyed the most, but when I was approached by North Bristol Institute for Adult Education, and asked if I would consider teaching French polishing and furniture restoration at one of their adult nightschool classes, I agreed straight away. Two hours a week from 7 p.m. till 9 p.m. on a Monday evening.

I ran the class for a number of years, starting at Monks Park on Gloucester Road. Then I moved to Bishop Road, and used the workshop where I spent so much time helping Mr Hody instead of attending music class. Finally the class was moved to Lockleaze School. Over the years I had met lots of different people; some became customers, some friends, and two in particular, approached me to see if I could put some work their way.

One of my students, a married woman named Pat, who was doing upholstery as a hobby, had starting buying Victorian chairs at auction and re-upholstering them to sell on. She had attended my restoration class to learn how to restore and repolish the chair frames before upholstering them.

We became friends, and her husband, who worked in re-placement windows, would sometimes let me have off-cuts of hardwood. When Pat learnt that I hated the process of stripping the old polish or varnish from furniture, she sensed another opportunity to earn some extra cash, and offered to undertake some work for me. We agreed a rate, and if I had a large re-polishing job come in she would help out.

Both Eileen and I would love to watch the expression on people's faces when we informed them that I employed a woman to strip for me.

Pat was actually an audio typist, so when I prepared notes on a particular process to hand out at nightschool, she would type them up for me to be duplicated, which shows how long ago this was. In fact, when we purchased our first computer with a word processer, my daughter came over to show me how to transfer my notes onto it, and made the chance remark, "crickey dad, you've got enough notes here to write a book!" Well that started something, didn't it!

The other student with whom Eileen and I became friendly, was a fireman named John, along with his wife Irene. I was helping put one of his projects into the back of his estate car after class one night, when he said that if I ever needed any help, he would be pleased to assist, stripping and polishing, anything really, even with pick-ups and deliveries.

I had noticed that of all the student I had taught over the years, John was by far the most talented, and it wasn't long before he and his wife Irene were taking more and more work off my hands. This was great, as not only had Eileen and I met and befriended two of the nicest people you could wish to meet, but I now had some help with pick ups and deliveries, and Irene was also becoming skilled at recaning chair seats.

John Cambridge

John eventually made a Victorian chair to match the three he had in his dining room, and was anxious to know what I thought of his effort. I told him hounestly, that it was every bit as good as I could have done myself. He had obviously had a good tutor, I told him. It was a cruel shock to learn that he had been diognosed with cancer, and he died just twelve months later.

One interesting turn of events that came about as a direct result of my teaching an adult night school class was being contacted by Radio Bristol. At that time there was a morning program called, Compass, that regularly feature a phone in where listeners could ring in and ask questions of experts on various subjects ranging from gardening to finance. The producer had asked an upholsterer and myself to answer questions on air about repairing furniture.

Now I know it didn't turn me into a celebrity broadcaster overnight, but it was a talking point for a while amongst friends.

At some point Mike began exporting 1930s English solid oak furiture to Germany, where it was in fashion at the time.

He would bring any of the pieces that needed repairing or repolishing to me, and load the van with my help outside my workshop in Alcove Road after the work had been done. It was a mutually beneficial arrangement. I had a flow of work coming in, and Mike had somewhere to store his furniture before it was loaded.

Loading for Germany with Mick and Robert, a young lad who was on a work experience scheme for a while.

On two or three occasions I accompanied him to Germany where we stayed with one of his regular customers. Then we would drive to Dortmund and set up a stall at an antiques market in Westfalenhallen.

Sometimes if he had a smaller load, he would use his Volvo estate rather than hire a van. With imaginative packing, such as fitting smaller items packed in boxes into drawers and cupboards, and sets of chairs inside wardrobes, it was astonishing how much could be carried on the roof of an estate car with strong suspension.

As is evident from a photograph I took at the German border check of one particularly large load. Customs officers at the post needed to be persuaded that the load was secure, before allowing us to pass.

Mike's Volvo at the German border

On one occasion when Mike visited my workshop, I had a Victorian mahogany dining table in for some minor repairs and repolishing, and I showed him where a shard of glass was embedded deep into the edge moulding. When my customer had pointed it out to me, I'd asked how it came to be there. I simply couldn't think of any way it could have occurred. It looked as if it had been literally hammered in like a nail.

I was equally astonished when I was informed that it had happened during an air raid, during the Bristol blitz. A high explosive bomb had blown in the window of the room the table was in, with such force that a glass shard had been embedded in the moulding of the table. Thankfully, my customer continued, nobody was sat at the table when it happened. Typically, after that, Mike always joked that if a dealer in Germany ever pointed out a mark or blemish on a piece of furniture in an effort to reduce the price, he would explain that it was bomb damage! I'm not sure I believed him.

1930s solid oak chair for the German market, being restored

Gradually, I found that even with my fireman friend John. who had now built himself a workshop at the bottom of his garden, I was finding it difficult not to keep my other customers waiting for some time. This was at a time when there were more and more people advertising that they restored antique furniture, and I was losing private clients without realising it.

When the day came that Mike no longer exported to Germany, I found I was seriously low on work, virtually overnight. I needed to earn some extra money from somewhere, and started looking in the job vacancy ads.

I even applied for a job in London with Plowden & Smith, who were looking for a new workshop manager for their furniture department. No ordinary job would have piqued my interest so far away, but Plowden & Smith were helping with the restoration of Windsor Castle, and advertised themselves at the time as, "By appointment to Her Majesty Queen Elizabeth II Restorers of Two and Three Dimensional Works of Art." I applied for the position, and was invited up for an interview.

During a tour of the various workshops I was impressed by the stardard of the work, the expertise, and the client list.

However, during lunch I spoke to a young man, a toner and gilder, who was working on restoring some of the water gilded items from the Windsor Castle fire.

Gold leaf is laid on top of layers of Gesso, (Whitting and glue size) and Bole, a fine slip clay. The colour or tone of the gilding depends upon the colour of the surface it's laid on, so matching new gilding to the original is a skill few possess. I don't believe there could have been more than a handful of people in the country who could have done his job, but how he managed to live on his salary inLondon I have no idea.

I could tell that my interview had gone well, and was asked how much I would expect in salary if offered the post. I was then told that I would hear in the next few days whether my application had been successful.

I later had a letter stating that they had been impressed by both my interview and the fact that I was already a member of BAFRA, The British Antique Restorers Association. However the salary I had requested was more than they currently paid their Heads of Departments.

THE BRITISH ANTIQUE FURNITURE RESTORERS' ASSOCIATION

This is to certify that

Colin Holcombe

is a Member of

the British Antique Furniture Restorers' Association

BAFRA Certificate

Of course while advertising in Yellow pages, various other potential clients would also get in touch. I remember driving down to Wells in Sommerset to polish a couple of very rare mechanical musical instruments.

A Phonoliszt-Violina is like a player piano, with changable punch cards for different tunes, that plays three violins at the same time.

The restorers in Wells had rebuilt the mechanical instruments and restored the cabinet work, but needed a french polisher who could match in the new work.

A Phonoliszt-Violina

Another time, Cowlins the construction contractors were moving to a new head office. The idea was to have a large board with their logo in the centre, surrounded by photographs of their current projects, in a prominent position in the foyer.. They wanted someone who could inlay the logo into an oak board using black walnut and affix moulded frames around it for the photographs.

I accepted the challenge and the result is shown below.

Project Board for Cowling's Head Office

I also received a call from Carlton Benbow, a firm of prestige shop-fitting contractors, who had the task of fitting out The Swallow Royal Hotel on College Green at the bottom of Park Street. It had previously been simply the Royal Hotel, but had been closed for some time. They wanted somebody local to repair any scratches that had been discovered during the snagging process, initially on items in the public areas such as the impressive reception desk shown here. There was too much work for one man, but a friend named Trevor had recently become unemployed and I enlisted his help, as well as that of Chris.

Trevor and Chris worked with me for several weeks at the Swallow Royal, and the work we carried out there must have been acceptable, as we were then asked to carry out the same tasks at another project for the Benbow group at New Westminster House in Baldwin Street, and later at the New Oxfordshire Golf Club in Thame.

Reception desk at the Swallow Royal Hotel

Three weeks work at the new Oxfordshire Golf Club in Thame

I first met Trevor after moving to Winterbourne and joining the tennis club, and getting to know some of the members socially. On my way home from night school class on a Monday evening I would pass a pub, and became aware that a car I recognised was always parked there.

Eileen named us The Good The Bad and The Ugly, but would never say which was which.

The owner of the car, Ken Budd, (on the right in the blue shirt above) would be there on a Monday night to have a drink with an old school friend of his, Trevor Harris, (in the middle.) and to cut a long story short, I started joining them on my way home from night school. This soon became a regular thing to do on a Monday, even when night school wasn't running.

Trevor had always been a keen collector of antiques, and he and his then wife Julia often visited antique markets and auctions in search of items for their cottage. Eventually, Trevor and I started a joint venture shipping antique furniture to Italy, and he would often help out on larger projects.

Trevor was a delight to work with on site, and soon joined in with the work ethic and banter that had developed between Chris and myself over the years. Chris and I would sometimes approach a project from a different angle, Chris from a carpenter or joiner's perspective, and myself from a cabinet maker or furniture restorer's perspective. Trevor, hearing Chris and I discussing various possible solutions to a problem, would often contribute to the discussion by making useful remarks such as, "Er..! what's going on er then?"

Things took an interesting new turn when Trevor, had finally stopped working as a noise analyst for the quarries, in favour of working with his hands, and had come to work in my workshop in Fishponds. He was contacted by a friend of his wife's family, an Italian living in Naples. This friend, Pino, had gone into partnership with another Italian, intent on establishing an antique business in Naples, selling primarily quality English mahogany Georgian and Victorian furniture.

They came over for a meeting with Trevor and myself, and proposed that Trevor and I should purchase the items they were looking for, restore them, and ship them over to an address in Naples. They would pay all the invoices and costs. The reason they wanted us to be involved was because they needed someone who knew about antiques with the ability to restore them, as well as somebody in England they knew they could trust.

The meeting took place at Trevor's cottage with his wife Julia, someone Pino would recognise. The business partner of Pino's looked like a sterotype mafia don, but sat and devouroured Julia's home made fruitcake as if he handn't eaten for days. To be honest, neither Trevor nor I were entirely sure what to make of him. Pino however came across as genuine enough. Trevor and I opened a business account, into which Pino would deposit money for us to spend purchasing furniture.

Trevor and I had a great time searching the auctions and purchasing the required stock; that was the easy bit. More difficult, was finding a company to ship a container of antique furniture to Naples! Now don't get me wrong, dealers had been shipping antiques abroad for years.

The trouble was not finding a shipping company, there were lots. The trouble was the destination. Typically, I would ring a company to ask if they would send a container of antiques abroad for us, and what the cost would be. They would then ask where the container was going, and as soon as I said Italy, it all changed. Some said Italy was the one country they didn't ship to, others said they would ship to Northern Italy, but would not go south of what was described as the Mafia Line. And one company said they used to ship to Italy, but no more, because there was still no sign of the last container they sent, its contents or the driver!

In the end however, we did manage to find a local shipping agent willing to undertake the task, and the first shipment went well. The problem was with the second load. Apparently all imports of antiques into Italy had to go to Milan first in order to go through some kind of custom check. Pino rang us, rather angry, to say that he had been fined the equivalent of £1,000. 00, for a false declaration of weight on the manifest, and that the load had been impounded until the fine was paid.

We rang the shipping company and were told that it was standard practice to estimate the weight of a container of furnitue, and that we should ring Customs and Excise. In the end I managed to speak to someone at Customs and Excise, who was sympathetic, and read out to me the EU regulations that stated, (False declaration of weight, No fine should be levied).
 When I pressed him further he admitted, "I know..but sometimes the Italians do levy a fine."

He went on to suggest that Pino should put in a claim for loss of earnings while the load was impounded, and demand the fine be repaid. Pino followed that advice but said that when he demanded a return of his fine, he was asked, "What fine?"

I was begining to see why Italy was such a difficult destination for shipping companies.

Chapter 10

My Book Shelf

The first print run was a hard cover editition.

I mentioned in the previous chapter, that it was a chance remark by my daughter about having enough notes for nightschool to write a book, that inspired me to do just that. I enlisted the aid of a friend who belonged to a camera club, and creating some rather simple illustrations in microsoft paint, I compiled a manuscript and sent it off to umpteen publishers.

After a plethera of rejections, The Crowood Press thought the manuscript worth publishing and a contract was signed. I would receive 10% of the publisher's net receipts and even received an advance of £750. I was very excited.

I had originally entitled the book, "Practical Repairs to Periode Furniture." However Crowood preferred to call it, simply, "How To Restore Antique Furniture."

When the book started to sell reasonably well in America, Crowood decided to produce a paper back edition.

They rang me up some time later, and announced that they were looking for someone to write a book on marquetry. As there was a chapter covering marquetry repairs in my first book, they wondered if I would write it for them.

Full of an exaggerated confidence in my ability to write such a book, after all, I was a published author, I readily agreed.

I had also enjoyed the process of transferring the knowledge I had acquired to print and sharing it with others, as well as drawing illustrations on the computor. I wanted to write another book.

The first one had been a huge boost to my confidence and self esteem, and gave me enormous bragging rights. When someone asked if I could do something on a particular day, I was able to say, with a rather smug smile, "I'm sorry, I have a meeting with my publisher that day."

When the contract came through for me to sign however, I began to realise the enormity of the task I had arrogantly committed myself to, however, and the smug smile soon departed.

I knew how to produce and restore antique saw cut marquetry, and in fact had explained the entire process of producing the elaborate panels in the maquetry cutter's workshop in my first book, which was the reason Crowood approached me.

I also realised that Crowood didn't want me to simply, expand on what I had already written. They wanted a book explaining how to produce artistic pictures and designs using the modern, thin, knife cut veneers, that had to be cut to shape, not with a saw, but with a craft-knife or scalpel. The book they wanted would be as much about the art of marquetry, not just the techniques involved, after all, there is a lot more to painting a portrait than simply knowing how to mix and apply paint to a canvas.

I knew little of this, and the contract stated that they wanted so many thousand words, a specified number of photographs, supplied as transparencies, and so many line drawing, all by a certain date.

This meant research! In my first book I hadn't needed to do any research, everything I needed to know was in my head.

This was different, I had some idea of what to do, but I needed help from someone well versed in the knife cut techniques and producing works of art with the somewhat limited palette on offer.

I enlisted the help of a local marquetry club and produced some pictures. However the illustrations were proving a problem with the limited software I had, The end result was a rushed, and I have to admit, rather poor book, that I was less than happy with. Nevertheless it was published, but only as a paperback, even for the first print run, a sure sign that the publishers weren't very thrilled with the result either.

The best thing about my second book was the cover

I was so disappointed with the job I had made of the book, that I hardly mentioned it to anyone.

Third book published by The Crowood Press An Introduction to Woodwork

Determined to prove that I could produce another, much better book, I began work on one. This time, I would do the same as with my first. Finish the book and be happy with the result, before any attempt to find a publisher.

I called the book, "An Introduction to Woodwork," and sent the manuscript to Crowood Press, and suprisingly, they once again agreed to publish.

I had a meeting with the head of their wood list, and learnt some interesting facts about the world of publishing. Firstly she explained that if she had been head of department at the time, she would never have approached me to write the marquetry book in the first place.

Not because I wasn't capable of writing it she explained, but simply because I was neither a celebrity, nor the winner of any award or marquetry competition, or the Director of Marquetry at some prestigious institute, if such a place even exists. If they commissioned a book on any subject, they would want someone who was well known, either for the subject matter itself, or a celebrity who had it as a hobby.

When I retired, I decided to continue writing books. Why? Well, It would keep me busy, and I enjoyed the process of writing a book and drawing the illustrations, even if I wasn't particularly good at it.

The idea of putting whatever knowledge I had gained over the years into print appealed to me, and after I had exhausted my knowledge of all things wood related, I saw no reason not to do the same with my other interests such as antique firearms and aviation.

The fact that I've not invested any money in promoting or advertising any of my books, means that very few have been sold, but at least writing them has, hopefully, delayed the onset of senillity for a while longer, that, along with doing the morning crossword.

I even thought I might have a go at writing a work of fiction. I'd had the idea for a crime thiller involving an antique dealer in my head for a long time, but I didn't think I was capable of writing a novel.

However, sat in front of the computor screen about to start another reference book, I thought to myself, why not give it a try? If I didn't give it a go, I would always wonder if I could have achieved it or not, so that's what I did. In the end I was pleased with the result and wrote and self published three more with the same characters.

They may not be as well written as a Stephen King, or a John Grisham, and they are certainly not works of literary brilliance, or ever likely to win any awards, or feature on the best seller list, but I believe them to be interesting and original stories, and easy to read. So at least I have the satisfaction of having done it, (four times now). It's for others to judge how well I did.

My four crime thrillers

In between writing crime novels, I purchased some software for the computor that enabled me to produce much better and more detailed illustrations for inclusion in my reference books, and I have at long last produced what I consider to be a far superior Marquetry book than the one I wrote for The Crowood Press.

Excited by the new illustrations I could produce, I decided to write three new books on wood related subjects, plus A History of Firearms, and a book on Aviation history, entitled The Story of Flight.

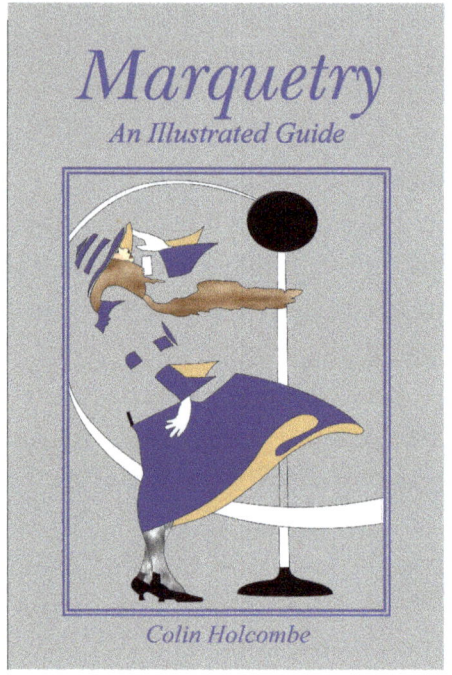

New Marquetry Book

 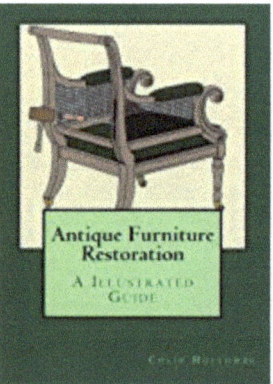 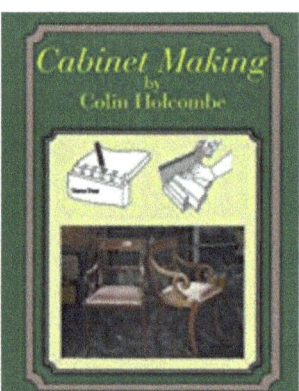

Three new wood related books

 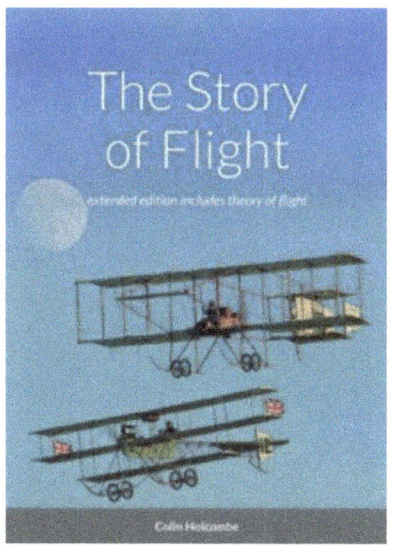

History of Firearms and The Story of Flight inspired two more books

Researching the life of Samuel Colt for "The History of Firearms," I realised just what an extraordinary man he had been, inspiring me to research his life in more detail. I discovered how his determination and flair for business made him wealthy, and also, how wealth is no protection from tragedy and heartbreak. I wrote, "Samuel Colt the Man Behind the Gun."

I was also amazed at the bravery of the early pioneers of aviation, and decided to write the incredible story of the race to be the first to fly from Britain to Australia in 1919. The story of the attempts by all six teams to fly such a distance, in open cockpits with unreliable engines, and over uncharted and often hostile forests, seas and deserts, where any forced landing would probably have ended in injury or death, shows just how courageous these men and women were.

 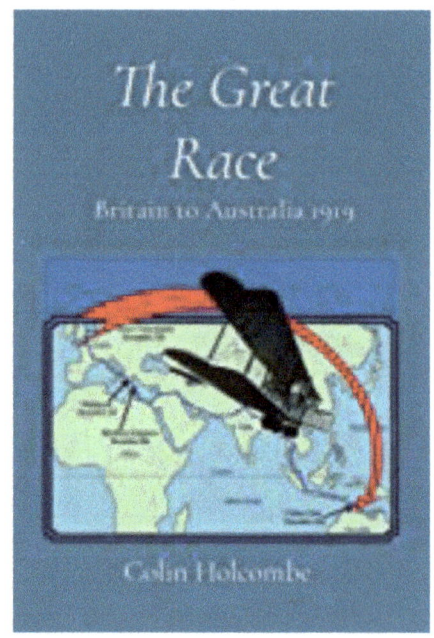

With these two books I enjoyed the research as much as the writing

Chapter 11

Cold War and the Bristol Bus Boycott

I finished school in 1963, the same year as the Bristol Bus Boycott, and this was the first time I'd really been made aware of racial discrimination in Bristol.

I'd had little contact with anyone of a different ethnic background during my school days, although there were two Sikh brothers attending St Michaels Junior Boys School while I was there, but the only reason they stand out in my memory is because of the way they wore their hair tied into a knot on the top of their heads, and one later wore a turban. At Bishop Road Secondary Modern I can only remember there being one black pupil, and he was in the year above me.

There were lots of jokes of course concerning the differences in cultures and outward appearance, but these stereotypes included all sorts, including the British, the French and the Italians. For instance, a Scotsman, an Irishman and an Englishman walk into a bar, and the barman asks...."Is this some kind of a joke?" I saw nothing wrong in it, any more than Dave Allan telling jokes about the difference between the Protestant and Catholic Church. Back then I think most people recognised that a joke about the difference between how an Englishman might react to a situation with his supposed "stiff upper lip" and an Italian with his "passionate nature" wasn't meant to be offensive, just amusing.

It was only when reading about the Bristol Bus Boycott, and seeing the protests outside the bus offices on the city centre, that I realised that it wasn't just about telling jokes, it was affecting peoples livelihoods, and could turn violent and nasty. I knew that some people who had lived through the war and lost friends and family members, bore grudges against their former enemies, but that wasn't because of skin colour or race, it was because they lost loved ones in the war. I understood the reason for that, but to refuse to employ someone purely because of their skin colour made no sense.

In the early 1960s Bristol had an estimated 3,000 residents of West Indian origin, some of whom had served in the British military during the Second World War. A large number of West Indian families lived in the area around City Road in St Pauls and had suffered discrimination. The community set up their own churches and associations, including the West Indian Association, which began to act as a representative body.

The Bristol Bus Boycot of 1963 arose from the refusal of the Bristol Omnibus Company to employ Black or Asian bus crews, although they were employed in lower paid positions in workshops and canteens. The Race Relations Act, which made racial discrimination unlawful in public places, wasn't passed until 1965, and the Act that extended the provisions to employment and housing didn't become law until 1968.

Four young West Indian men, Roy Hackett, Owen Henry, Audley Evans and Prince Brown, formed an action group, later to be called the West Indian Development Council. They were unhappy with the lack of progress in fighting discrimination by the West Indian Association. The group asked Paul Stephenson, an articulate college graduate who Owen Henry had met, and whose father was from West Africa, to be their spokesman.

Stephenson set up a test case to prove that a colour bar existed by arranging an interview with the bus company for Guy Bailey, a young warehouseman and Boys' Brigade officer. When Stephenson told the company that Bailey was West Indian, the interview was cancelled. Inspired by the refusal of Rosa Parks to give up her seat on a bus in Alabama and the ensuing bus boycott in Montgomery USA in 1955, the activists decided on a bus boycott in Bristol.

Their action was announced at a press conference on 29 April 1963. The following day, they claimed that none of the city's West Indians were using the buses and that many white people supported them.

Students from Bristol University held a protest march to the bus station in support of the boycott and many leading politions, including Tony Benn, spoke out against the colour bar.

The boycott of the company's buses by Bristolians lasted for four months until the company finally backed down and overturned their discriminative colour bar policy.

Unite, the successor to the Transport and General Workers Union, issued an apology in February 2013, and Laurence Faircloth, the union's South West secretary said of the union's stance at the time, "it was completely unacceptable. I can well accept the sense of injustice and pain that has been felt because of what happened in Bristol all those years ago".

In the 2009 New Years Honours, Stephenson was appointed an Officer of the Order of the British Empire (OBE) for his part in organising the bus boycott, and Roy Hackett and Guy Bailey were also made OBEs for their services to Equal Opportunities and to Community Relations in Bristol.

All three received OBEs

I mentioned that when working at Hall & Rohan we carried out work for the Merchant Venturers and the Georgian House in Great George Street. 7 Great George Street was the home of the Pinney family. John Pinney owned slaves who worked on his lands in the New World, and brought two slaves over from Nevis in the West Indies, to work as house servants when he and his family moved back to England.

It was unusual to bring slaves to England as Pinney did, probably because you could employ an English servant, who already spoke English and understood the customs. It was a small wage anyway. and it would have been more economical to do so, rather than bringing a slave over on a long sea journey, who would have to be taught, not just his or her duties, but to speak English.

One such slave however was Pero Jones. Pero and another house servant, the freed slave Frances Coker, accompanied the family in their move from Nevis to England in 1783 and to Bristol in 1784. Pero was personal servant to John Pinney, and Frances was lady's maid to Jane Pinney. Pero was trained as a barber, and on Nevis he was often entrusted with large amounts of cash. Both "servants" visited Nevis in 1790 and Pero visited again in 1794.

According to Pinney, after this last visit, Pero seemed to change, and started to drink heavily and his behaviour became a matter of concern. Pinney wondered if something happened during this visit to Nevis to bring about this change?

The Georgian House. home of the Pinney family

When Pero fell ill in 1798, Pinney decided that a change of air would be beneficial, so Pero was sent to Ashton, out in the country to convalesce, and Pinney and his family visited him there often. Pero was about 45 when he died, and had served the Pinney family for 32 years. Reading the family papers that are on show, it's obvious that the family were fond of Pero, and as far as we know, although treated *almost* as one of the family, he was never given his freedom, and died a slave.

Furniture that I may have worked on in the Georgian House

I remember picking up a piece of furniture from the Georgian House that both Pinney and Pero would also have handled, when I was working for Hall & Rohan. The Georgian bookcase with the thirteen pane tracery doors and broken pediment were typical of the type of furniture we worked on.

In March 1999, a new footbridge across the River Frome in Bristol harbour was named after Pero, in commemoration of one slave who lived and died in the city.

Pero's Bridge

The bridge is composed of three spans, the two outer ones are fixed, but the central section can be raised to provide a navigation channel in the harbour.

Pero's Bridge with centre span lifted

The most distinctive features of the bridge are the pair of horn-shaped sculptures which act as counterweights for the centre section when lifted.

Another well-known black servant in Bristol was Scipio Africanus. He worked for Charles Williams, the Earl of Suffolk, at the Great House at Henbury. Scipio died aged 18 in 1720 and he was buried nearby at St Mary's church. For some reason, his burial was not recorded in the parish register. However, his grave is marked by ornate gravestones which describe his conversion to Christianity.

Grave of Scipio Africanus

Enslaved Africans were usually given new names, often their "*owners*"" surnames. Some were given grand names, which in fact emphasised their lower status: Scipio for example, was named after the noted Roman general.

There are fewer records of black people coming to Bristol after the slave trade was abolished in 1807, although Bristol merchants continued to trade with West Africa in goods such as palm oil.

An unusual record from St Mary Redcliffe church shows that West African trading partners sometimes sent their sons to be educated in Britain. Augustine Manga Bell was baptised in 1868 and described as "*Augustine Manga Bell son of King Bell of Cameron (Cameroon), Native Chief*"

When I and my friends passed our driving tests, we all managed to do so at the first attempt at the age of seventeen, which was just as well, because the amount of ribbing anyone who failed would have received would have been painfut to see. I've already mentioned in chapter five, that my first car was a Vauxhall Victor. It was purchased from Runway Garage on the A38 in Patchway, at a cost of £120/ 0s / 0d. Runway Garage had been relocated from it's original location at the end of Filton runway in 1962. The relocation came about because, in the 1950s and early '60s, Filton was designated as a V bomber dispersal base, and during the Cuban Missile Crisis (October 1962) Avro Vulcan V bombers were located at Filton and kept at "immediate readiness" status with engines idling.

One incident of note involved a Avro Vulcan which arrived at the airfield from the west, and in heavy rain. As it touched down and the brakes were applied, the aircraft aquaplaned along the wet tarmac. The pilot quickly decided to abort the landing and applied full power for a take-off instead. Although the abortive manoeuvre was successful, unfortunately as the aircraft gained height the jet blast extensively damaged the Petrol Station at the eastern end of the runway, and eye-witnesses reported seeing cars spinning everywhere on the A38 trunk-road. I'm sure the eye witness reports were somewhat exaggerated, but the consequences of the incident could have been much worse   The fuel station was subsequently relocated out of harms way.

Runway Garage before relocation

The only time I have personally observed a Vulcan bomber in flight was at an airshow in Weston-s-Mare with Alan Peglar around 1960.

Vulcan at the airshow with bomb doors open

This was when pilots could fly close to the watching crowds. It flew close over our heads in a banking turn with it's bomb doors open, so that we had a clear view of the bomb bay.

One incident that took place that happened during my last year of school on the 2nd Secember 1962. A Vulcan bomber was being used as a test-bed for the Olypus 320 engine at Filton, when the shaft failed and the whole turbine was thrown off, cutting the airframe in half and setting the aircraft alight.

As the airframe and the Olypus engine both contained magnesium alloy, observers recalled that,"the whole thing went up like a firework display." When wing collapsed due to the heat, it allowed burning oil to run down the runway and ebgulf the BAC fire appliance that was in attendance and it to was engulfed by fire and utterly destroyed.

Impression of the test-bed fire
Julian Cheek

During the sixties we were keen on not just planes and spies, but political satire as well. There was an American magazine that was popular at the time called MAD. We didn't know it at the time but it was called MAD because the original Mad head office was initially located in Lower Manhattan at 225 Lafayette Street, while in the early nineteen sixties it moved to 485 Madison Avenue, the location listed in the magazine as, 485 MADison Avenue.

However, this was the sixties and the Cold War ensured that the initials MAD meant something completely different to us.

We knew it as the name of the Cold War nuclear defence policies of the sixties.

Both Russian and American nuclear defence relied upon the fact that if either side launched it's intercontinental ballistic missiles in a pre-emptive first strike, the other side's early warning system, would mean they could still launch their arsenol of weapons before their missile silos were destroyed, ensuring the complete destruction of both sides, no matter who fired first Thus, the appropriately named MAD, (Mutual Assured Destruction.)

This is why almost the entire world held its breath, when images taken by one of the American U-2 spy planes, showed that the Russians were setting up nuclear launch sites on the island of Cuba.

We knew all about U-2 spy planes because, on 1st May 1960, a United States U-2 spy plane was shot down by the Soviet Air Defence Forces while conducting photographic aerial reconnaissance deep inside Soviet territory. The aircraft, flown by American pilot Francis Gary Powers, crashed near Sverdlovsk (present-day Yekaterinburg). Powers parachuted to the ground safely and was captured.

The incident occurred during the tenures of American president Dwight D. Eisenhower and Soviet leader Nikita Khrushchev, around two weeks before the scheduled opening of an east–west summit in Paris, France. Krushchev and Eisenhower had met face-to-face at Camp David in Maryland in September 1959, and the seeming thaw in U.S.-Soviet relations had raised hopes globally for a peaceful resolution to the Cold War. The U2 incident shattered the amiable "Spirit of Camp David" that had prevailed for eight months, prompting the cancellation of the summit in Paris and causing great embarrassment to the U.S. on the international stage. The Pakistani government issued a formal apology to the Soviet Union for its role in the U-2 mission.

Following his capture, Powers was convicted of espionage and sentenced to three years of imprisonment plus seven years of hard labour; he was released two years later, in February 1962, in a prisoner exchange for Soviet intelligence officer Rudolf Abel.

Lockheed U-2 spy plane

America, under the presidency of John F. Kennedy could not allow Russian missiles sites to be established on Cuba, so close to the American coast, because a pre-emptive strike from there would have meant that America would not have enough warning to retaliate, especially as the early warning network was set up to detect missiles arriving from the north over Alaska.

When this was reported to President John F. Kennedy, he convened a meeting of the nine members of the National Security Council and five other key advisers, in a group that became known as the Executive Committee of the National Security Council (EXCOMM).

During this meeting, President Kennedy was originally advised to carry out an air strike on Cuban soil in order to compromise Soviet missile supplies, followed by an invasion of the Cuban mainland.

Thankfully, after careful consideration, Kennedy chose a less aggressive course of action, in order to avoid a declaration of war. Kennedy ordered a naval "quarantine" on October 22 to prevent further missiles from reaching Cuba. By using the term "quarantine", rather than "blockade" (an act of war by legal definition), the United States was able to avoid the implications of a state of war.

The US announced it would not permit offensive weapons to be delivered to Cuba and demanded that the weapons already in Cuba be dismantled and returned to the Soviet Union.

After several days of tense negotiations, an agreement was reached between Kennedy and Khrushchev: publicly, the Soviets would dismantle their offensive weapons in Cuba and return them to the Soviet Union, subject to United Nations verification, in exchange for a US public declaration and agreement to not invade Cuba. Secretly, the United States agreed with the Soviets that it would dismantle all of the Jupiter MRBMs which had been deployed to Turkey against the Soviet Union.

The blockade was formally ended on November 20th. The negotiations between the United States and the Soviet Union pointed out the necessity of a quick, clear, and direct communication line between the two superpowers. As a result, the Moscow–Washington hotline was established. A series of agreements later reduced US–Soviet tensions for several years, until both parties eventually resumed expanding their nuclear arsenals.

It later emerged that the US Navy had dropped a series of "signalling" depth charges (practice depth charges the size of hand grenades) on a Soviet submarine (*B-59*) at the blockade line, unaware that it was armed with a nuclear-tipped torpedo with orders that allowed it to be used if the submarine was damaged by depth charges or surface fire.

As the submarine was too deep to monitor any radio traffic the captain of the *B-59*, Valentin Grigoryevich Savitsky, decided that a war might already have started and wanted to launch a nuclear torpedo.

The decision to launch these normally only required agreement from the two commanding officers on board, the Captain and the Political Officer. However, the commander of the submarine Flotilla, Vasily Arkhipov, was aboard *B-59* and so he also had to agree. Arkhipov objected and so the nuclear launch was narrowly averted.

On the same day a U-2 spy plane made an accidental, unauthorised ninety-minute overflight of the Soviet Union's far eastern coast.

The Soviets responded by scrambling MiG fighters from Wrangel Island; in turn, the Americans launched F-102 fighters armed with nuclear air-to-air missiles over the Bering Sea.

Although the world was holding it's breath, I doubt that anyone realised just how close we had come to a full scale nuclear war!

U S Navy Helicopter hovers over a Soviet submarine

Where were you when Kennedy was shot? That's the question that everyone of my generation gets asked at some time or another, and nearly all of us can remember, much like the moon landings, and of course more recently the attack on the Twin Towers in New York. These incidents give rise to so many conspiracy theories. And I do love a good conspiracy theory.

Let me start with the first and most frequently asked. On November 22, 1963, I was sat watching televison in the front room of 6 Chandos Road with my father, my mother was probably preparing food for us all in the kitchen, when my brother come home and asked excitedly "Have you been watching the news?"

"No...why?" was dad's reply

"Kennedy's been shot...put the news on!"

President John F. Kennedy was the youngest and most popular president America has had, and certainly the first I took any interest in, mainly because he was determined to put a man on the moon.

He announced, "We choose to go to the Moon in this decade and do the other things, not because they are easy, but because they are hard; because that goal will serve to organize and measure the best of our energies and skills."

After the Second World War, anyone who had made use of slave labour was legally a war criminal, however the Russians, the Americans and the British were anxious to recruit German scientists and especially rocket scientists, into their rocket development and space programmes, so few of those were prosecuted.

Alan and myself followed the space race between Russia and America with enthusiasm.

On Oct. 4, 1957, the Soviets launched the first artificial satellite, Sputnik 1, into space. Four years later on April 12, 1961, Russian Lt. Yuri Gagarin became the first man in space as he orbited Earth in Vostok 1. His flight lasted 108 minutes, and Gagarin reached an altitude of 327 kilometers (about 202 miles).

First man in space Yuri Gagarin

The first U.S. satellite, Explorer 1, went into orbit on Jan. 31, 1958, and in 1961, Alan Shepard became the first American to fly into space. On Feb. 20th 1962, John Glenn's historic flight made him the first American to orbit the Earth. Both these missions were part of the Mercury project, there being only just enough room in the capsule for one astronaught.

Both Alan and myself purchased models of the Saturn V rocket, and were devastated by the news that three Apollo astronauts had been killed in a cabin fire during a launch pad test in 1967. However, just over two years later, on July 20th 1969, we were glued to the television screen watching the moon landing.

After some of the images taken from the moon were shown for the first time, the one that captured our imagination the most, was of the Earth rising over the horizon. I still think it's an astonishing sight.

Earthrise

Although I continued to be interested in all that was going on with the moon missions, public interest had waned. The launch of another rocket to the moon was common place, it might not even make the front page.

Apollo 13 changed all that, and the world was once again glued to news updates. There had been an explosion in the command module, and it looked as if the astronauts may not make it back.

Abandoning the mission to save their lives, the astronauts climbed into the Lunar Module and were slingshot around the Moon to speed their return back to Earth.

It was an amazing survival story that had the whole world glued to the news channels. We had the news on all day to be kept up to date with what was being done.

If anyone gets a chance to watch the film "Apollo 13", they should do so. You might be tempted to think the film makers have over dramatised it, but the actual events were far more dramatic.

On July 26th 1971 Apollo 15 launched with better life-support equipment, and a Lunar Roving Vehicle built by Boeing to explore the Moon.

The Luna Rover

That's right, they put a car on the moon, so the astronauts could cover more ground.

No sour grapes on my part when I say that, The "Boeing Luna Rover Ghia." Four wheel drive, off road, solar powered vehicle is still up there, and unlike any of my cars, it will still be in showroom condition, and I'll bet it hasn't depreciated in value one penny! !

Chapter 12

Bristol's Legacy

Monty Phyton fans will remember the scene in, The Life of Brian, when Reg, the character played by the brilliant John Cleese, a former pupil of Clifton College in Bristol, asks the question "What have the Romans ever done for us?" to which it emerges, quite a lot, roads the viaduct, etc.

Instead, Reg could have asked, "What has Bristol ever done for us?" And received the following replies.

Blankets:

Thomas Blanket was one of many Flemish weavers invited over to England by King Edward III in 1327 because he wanted England's vast cloth industry to expand. We had the sheep, but exported the wool. Blanket set up in Bristol, and got into a spot of bother with the local merchants because he started bringing together all the hand weavers under one roof, cutting overheads and creating a factory like process. The King backed him, however, and soon, affordable, mass-produced, tightly woven woollen covers that people could afford. were being made in large numbers. They were called blankets.

I've already mentioned Bristol Cream Sherry and Bristol Blue Glass, as well as many well known Bristol landmarks, but one buildng I haven't mentioned is the strange tower I remember my father pointing out to me in Bristol that he called the shot tower.

Lead shot:

The Shot Tower

Until sometime around 1780 the lead shot used in firearms was irregular in shape, because nobody knew how to make large quantities of it round, and this was a huge disadvantage because it would fly off in all directions.

A plumber by the name of William Watts, had noticed that if molten lead fell from a roof and landed in a bucket of cold water it would invariably form a round ball.

Watts dug a cellar under his house in Redcliffe, and a three storey tower on the roof. and patented his idea in 1782.

His invention resulted in much more accurate guns, and provided ball bearings for a range of industrial and engineering applications. There is still a post war shot tower, although no longer in use, in the area today.

The Plimsole Line

A line to mark the safe loading level on the side of a ship had been used since the Middle Ages, and in 1835 Lloyds safe levels became known as "Lloyd's Rule."

However, in the 1860 ships were still being lost due to overloading. Bristol born MP, Samuel Plimsole took up the case and in 1876 the United Kingdom Shipping Act made the load line compulsory, and in 1906, laws were passed requiring foreign ships visiting Bristol ports to be marked with the load or Plimsole line.

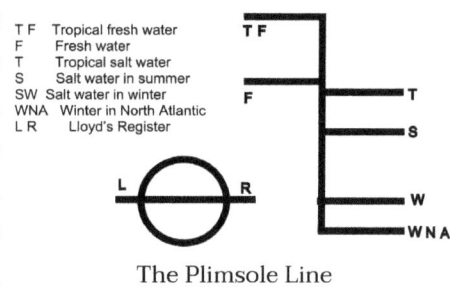

The Plimsole Line

Pirates and treasure maps

Of course, there have been pirates ever since people started crossing the seas, but when the world thinks of the classic image of a pirate, it's one that has come straight down the Avon Gorge.

Many of the great pirates of folklore were real and from Bristol - people like John Rackham, better known as Calico Jack, Israel Hands - the real one, not the one from Treasure Island - and of course Edward Thatch, better known as Blackbeard.

Their dress, accent, style and mannerisms are what anyone dressing up as a pirate for Talk Like A Pirate Day will copy, and it's straight out of Bristol.

The Llandoger Trow
Bristol City Archives Ref: 40826/BUI/50.

A lot of that also has to do with the way their facts transferred into fiction, from Robert Louis Stevenson's Treasure Island through to Robert Newton's portrayal of Long John Silver in the 1950 film version.

The pub, The Llandoger Trow, is said to have inspired Robert Louis Stevenson to write of the Admiral Benbow Inn in Treasure Island and Daniel Defoe supposedly met Alexander Selkirk there, who was his inspiration for Robinson Crusoe.

The pub is also supposedly haunted, with up to 15 ghosts, the best known being a small child whose footsteps can be heard on the top floor.

Laughing Gas

Nitrous oxide was first synthesised in 1772 by English natural philosopher and chemist Joseph Priestley, who called it phlogisticated nitrous air. The first practical use of the gas was made by Thomas Beddoes and James Watt who jointly published a book entitled, "Considerations on the Medical Use and on the Production of Factitious Airs," in 1794.

Clinical trials started in 1798 when Thomas Beddoes established a, Pneumatic Institution for Relieving Diseases by Medical Airs, in Hotwells in Bristol, England, under the supervision of a young Humphrey Davy. Davy discovered that inhalation of nitrous oxide could relieve a person of pain, but despite his discovery, it was another forty-four years before doctors used it for anaesthesia.

The institute lasted less than two years, scuppered by a typhoid outbreak, but the advances in medicine, notably in equipment and the potential for gas to be used as an anaesthetic were taken to London by Humphrey Davy, and many are still in use today.

Aircraft Design and manufacture

Bristol has contributed so much to aircraft development that it's hard to know where to begin. So I'll start with the first I knew of. The Brabazon.

As I've mentioned, my father was reluctant to talk about his wartime experiences, but would, sometimes talk about Filton and the Brabazon, and the village of Charlton.

As early as 1943 a committee had been formed to plan for post-war civil aviation. Chaired by J T C Moore-Brabazon M.C. it worked on the assumption that the Allies would be victorious in the war. At first, the Bristol Aeroplane Company (BAC) was not among the group of aircraft manufacturers who were invited to join the consultation but after protests, Leslie Frise, (designer of the Bristol Beaufighter and the Frise Aileron) was invited to attend the first meeting on January 14th 1943 in London.

One of the committee's recommendations was for a large transatlantic airliner and BAC was asked to look into it, provided that it didn't interfere with the company's important war work.

Construction of the Brabazon prototype began in October 1945 and was planned along the lines of the pre-war Imperial Airways flying boats with an onboard cinema, lounge bar and sleeping quarters for around 100 1st class passengers.

Being 54 metres long with a wingspan of 70 metres, the Brabazon required a stronger and longer runway than other aircraft of the time, not just for normal take-offs but also in case of emergency landings and brake failures. This meant that the existing runway at the BAC Filton works had to be lengthened.

The three-bay Brabazon Hangar was built, and the hangar doors and the railway level crossing for the aircraft were the largest in the world at the time. After a worker was crushed and killed while taking a sleep in one of the folds of the hangar doors, a siren was installed to warn employees when the doors were being operated.

It was agreed that the village of Charlton, comprising of some 88 homes, a public house and a post office and which was adjacent to the airfield, would have to be demolished, and the existing residents re-housed in council accommodation in Patchway, paying a subsidised rent.

It is said that construction of the extended runway used so much cement that it caused a shortage in the South West of England. Eventually the runway, although only seeing limited use with the Brabazon, proved an enormous asset for BAC with their future projects. As a Bristolian and aviation enthusiast, I find it sad to see the Filton runway unused, large areas of the airfield sold off for housing, and now proposals for the Brabazon hanger becoming a music venue.

The Bristol Brabazon outside its specially built hanger

The Brabazon was powered by a total of eight Bristol Centaurus 18-cylinder radial engines, the most powerful British-built piston engines available at the time, each being capable of generating 2,650 hp. These engines were installed in a unique arrangement where each was paired with another, but instead of sharing a common crankshaft, the paired engines each had their driveshafts angled towards an enormous central gearbox. Between them they drove a series of eight paired contra-rotating propellers which were set on four forward-facing nacelles.

The maiden flight, piloted by Chief Test Pilot Bill Pegg, took place on the 4th September 1949 and on 15th June 1950, the aircraft gave demonstration flights at London Airport.

Brabazon was destined to be the wrong aircraft at the wrong time however. Airline companies were looking to move into the jet age and in America, manufacturers were busy converting their large bombers into civil airliners with great success and were meeting the current demand. Unable to find buyers, BAC sold the only existing Brabazon for scrap after it had completed only 400 hours flying time.

The Brabazon had not been a commercial success but neither was it a complete loss. The research and manufacturing experience gained in building and flying such a large technically advanced aircraft were invaluable to BAC. The lessons about pressurised cabins, hydraulic power controls, electrical generation and engine controls were later used on the development of several other aircraft.

Runway extention at Filton

As far as I was aware at that time there were two other airfields in Bristol besides Filton. The main civil Airport at Lulsgate, and a smaller airport at Whitchurch. Whitchurch Airport was a municipal airport also known as (Bristol Whitchurch Airport) and was located just a few miles south of the city centre, and operated between 1930 and 1957.

It was in fact the main airport for Bristol and the surrounding area. During World War Two, it was one of the few civil airports in Europe that remained operational, enabling air connections to Lisbon and Shannon and onwards to the United States.

It all started in 1929, when the Corporation of the City of Bristol bought 298 acres of farmland to the south of the city, near Whitchurch, with the intention of building a new municipal airport.

On 31st May 1930, the airport was officially opened by Prince George, Duke of Kent, and in its first year of operation, the airport handled 915 passengers, soon growing to over 4,000 by 1939. The Bristol and Wessex Aeroplane Club relocated there from Filton Airfield, and together with Bristol Corporation, managed the facilities. The first buildings were a hangar, a clubhouse for the flying club, and an aircraft showroom.

Early services were an "air ferry" to Cardiff, operated by Norman Edgar & Co. and flights to Torquay and Teignmouth. By 1932, two air taxi firms were based at the airport, and by 1934, Bristol Air Taxis was joined by Railway Air Services, a subsidiary of Imperial Airways, offering connections to Plymouth, Birmingham, London, Southampton and Liverpool.

In July 1935, a new terminal building was opened, and regular international services started.

Bristol Whitchurch Airport
Bristol City Archives Ref: 40826/AIR/3

In 1936 Norman Edgar moved to the new airport at Weston-super-Mare. The company had been renamed Norman Edgar (Western Airways) Ltd, and in 1938 it was taken over by Whitney Straight who renamed it Western Airways, Ltd.

In 1937, Irish Sea Airways (later to become Aer Lingus), and Great Western and Southern Airlines commenced operations from Whitchurch.

In July 1938, the prospect of war with Germany prompted the Government to form a Civil Air Guard to train pilots for the forthcoming hostilities.

The Bristol and Wessex Aeroplane Club was one of the training organisations enlisted in this effort, and in addition No. 33 Elementary and Reserve Flying Training School was established at Whitchurch. The tragic death of Frank Barnwell, the chief designer for BAC at Filton, in an accident when taking off, ended the life of a man who had given us the The Bristol Scout, The Bristol Fighter, the Bristol Bulldog and The Bristol Blenheim.

In late August 1939, the airport was requisitioned by the Air Ministry, and was declared a Restricted Area. British Airways Ltd and Imperial Airways were at this time joining together to form the British Overseas Airways Cororation (BOAC), and were ordered to Bristol Whitchurch Airport to undertake wartime transport work. Civil flights resumed again later in the year, after an east-west runway and taxiways were built, and in September 1940 aircraft belonging to the Dutch Airline, KLM were based at Whitchurch after escaping the German invasion of the Netherlands, and operated flights to Lisbon under a BOAC charter.

On 1 June 1943, BOAC Flight 777 was shot down en route to Whitchurch from Lisbon, with the loss of four Dutch crew and 13 passengers, including the actor Leslie Howard. It has been suggested that the flight was targeted because the Germans suspected that Winston Churchill was on board.

Not long after the war, the increase in air traffic rendered the site too small for airlines to be based there, so it was decided to move to the RAF base at Lulsgate Bottom in May 1957 which became Bristol Airport.

Since then the former airfield has been home to a Formula Two racing circuit, a sports centre, trading estates and retail parks, and the South Bristol Community Hospital opened on the site in 2012, taking over the responsibility for the patients transferred there from the Bristol General Hospital.

The Bristol Boxkite

Bristol's contribution to the development of aircraft and engine design began when George White first heard of the Wright brothers' achievement. He decided to turn his interest in aviation into a commercial business. He was well versed in the transportation business, and although not an engineer himself he was running several businesses.

At the Annual General Meeting of one of his companies, the "Bristol Tramways & Carriage Company," in 1910 he announced that he had registered the names of four new companies, Bristol Aeroplane Company Limited, British & Colonial Aeroplane Company Limited, Bristol Aviation Company Limited and British & Colonial Aviation Company Limited.

George White chose to operate initially as the British & Colonial Aeroplane Company rather than use the name Bristol, in case it proved difficult to register as a trade mark. He set up the head office in Clare Street House, Bristol, which was also home to some of his other companies - George White & Co. Stockbrokers, the Western Wagon & Property Company Limited, Bristol Tramways & Carriage Company Limited and Imperial Tramways Company Limited.

The manufacturing workshops were based initially in two sheds leased from the Tramways company at their depot in Filton, just north of Bristol. Most aeroplane companies at that time were being set up by designers and engineers who struggled to get funding. George White on the other hand was a wealthy businessman, willing to invest heavily in his new venture, and by February 1913 the share capital of the business had risen to £250,000, enough to cover the expansion of the Filton site.

The idea was to build a Farmen aircraft under licience, but an engineer at Filton believed he could build an improved copy by incorporating elements of another aircraft, and the Bristol Boxkite was born. Farmen sued Bristol but dropped the case when lawyers pointed out the design improvements.

Between 11th and 16th November a series of demonstration flights of the new Bristol Boxkite were made in Bristol.

Temporary hangars were built for the aircraft on Durdham Down, Bristol,

Although flying was limited by the weather conditions, a crowd of almost 10,000 saw Maurice Tetard make a fifteen-minute flight on the Saturday.

That first flight was soon eclipsed by some spectacular flights made the following Tuesday, when around ten flights were made between 7 and 9 o'clock, including a fifteen-minute flight by Tetard, during which he flew over Clifton Suspension Bridge, and made a circuit over the Bristol suburbs of Redland and Westbury.

Tetard flying over the Clifton Suspension bridge

On 14th March 1911, the British War Office ordered four Bristol Boxkites for the planned Air Battalion Royal Engineers, the first production contract for military aircraft for Britain's armed forces. The first Boxkite, powered by a 50 hp Gnome engine, was delivered to Larkhill on 18th May that year. An order for a further four Boxkites was placed later that year, for use mainly as a trainer.

As it was used by Bristol for instruction purposes at their flying schools at both Larkhill and Brooklands, many early British aviators would have learned to fly in a Bristol Boxkite. Four were purchased in 1911 by the War Office and examples were sold to Russia and Australia. It continued to be used for training purposes until after the outbreak of the First World War.

The first Boxkites to be built had upper and lower wings of equal span, although most of the aircraft eventually produced had an extended upper wing and were known as the Military Version.

Boxkite on army manoeuvres on Salisbury Plain 1911
Bristol City Archives Ref: 40826/AIR/8

My own memories of the Boxkite are from when my friend Alan and I would visit the City Museum, a favourite if the weather was unpleasant and a facinating place, full of unusual exhibits, including a replica boxkite hanging over the main hall.

Replica Boxkite in the main hall of the Bristol Museum

But the Boxkite was only the first of so many aircraft designed and built in Bristol.

During the 1950s, the government required the aviation industry to consolidate. In consequence only two engine makers were left by 1959, Rolls-Royce and Bristol Siddeley. From 1959 to 1961 the British government forced the consolidation of a further twenty or so British aviation firms, including Vickers and English Electric's aviation interests, into three larger groups with the threat of withheld contracts and the lure of project funding. While the majority of fixed-wing aircraft design and construction lay with the British Aircraft Corporation and the Hawker Siddeley Group, the helicopter divisions of Bristol, Fairey and Saunders-Roe, with their hovercraft, were merged with Westland to form Westland Helicopters in 1961.

Hawker Siddeley later merged with BAC in 1977

The British government was in control of route-licensing for private airlines, and also oversaw the newly established and publicly owned British Overseas Airways Corporation (BOAC) for long-range flights and the British European Airways (BEA) for short and medium-range flights.

Bristol Britannia

In the early fifties, BOAC required an airliner that could take off from short runways in order to service its long-haul Empire routes and Bristol built the Britannia airliner to fulfil these requirements.

The first pair of prototypes were powered by the early series Proteus 625 engine. This was the direct follow-up to the 600 series engine that had already successfully completed its type trials, having been originally designed to replace the piston engines on the Brabazon.

The maiden flight took place on August 16th 1952 with Chief Test Pilot Bill Pegg at the controls, and turned out to be a rather eventful one. The over-sensitive flying controls led to a wild pitching before Pegg managed to regain control. During the landing approach, smoke filled the cockpit and the main undercarriage bogie was stuck in its cycle, only fully deploying seconds before landing. These "snags" however, proved to be minor and by September, the prototype was cleared to perform at the 1952 SBAC (Society of British Aerospace Companies) display at Farnborough, where spectators commented on the "quietness" of the giant airliner, leading to it becoming known as "The Whispering Giant.

However, in 1953 and 1954, after the crash of the three de Havilland Comets, the Air Ministry demanded that the Britannia undergo lengthy tests. Further delays still were attributed to teething problems with the engine, and in February 1954, Bill Pegg was flying the second prototype, G-ALRX, with potential buyers from KLM on board, when an engine fire, caused by a failed reduction gear, threatened to engulf the entire wing. Bill Pegg was concerned that the intense heat could melt the main spar so he took the decision to land on the mud flats on the Severn Estuary. In his autobiography he says, "*Whilst we succeeded in putting out the first fire by turning off the fuel, the fire-extinguisher system failed to cope with the oil tank blaze."* Needless to say, KLM did not purchase any Britannia aircraft.

Britannia after landing on the mud flats

I was still in infant school when all this was taking place, but even I can remember my father telling us about it over breakfast, when reading the news paper report.

Issues of icing were highlighted by BOAC after they had taken delivery of the Britannia and although this problem was easily overcome by simply selecting a different cruising height to the one specified, they were exaggerated publicly by the company, who had now changed their mind and wanted the Boing 707 instead of Britannia, virtually killing off its sales prospects. The Britannia was retired in 1975 and only 85 were ever built. It's probable that sales to other companies would have been few anyway, simply because the Britannia was designed specifically for the needs of one company, BOAC, and didn't necessarily meet the needs of others, the result possibly of too much government control. Other companies were more generally competitive, designing aircraft to meet the needs of many airlines, not just one, with a view to overall sales.

Bristol Blenheim

1935 saw the first flight of the Blenheim built in Bristol by the Bristol Aeroplane Company, formerly the British and Colonial Aeroplane Company. The Blenheim was a light bomber aircraft design and was used throughout the Second World War, especially in the first two years. The aircraft was developed as *Type 142*, a civil airliner, in response to a challenge from Lord Rothermere, to produce the fastest commercial aircraft in Europe. The *Type 142* first flew in April 1935, and the Air Ministry, impressed by its performance, ordered a modified design as the *Type 142M* for the Royal Air Force as a bomber. Deliveries of the newly named Blenheim to RAF squadrons commenced on 10th March 1937.

Bristol Beaufighter:

The Bristol Beaufighter, nicknamed "Whispering Death" by the Japanese, was a versatile long-range fighter devised for both offensive and defensive roles.

In October 1938 at an Air Ministry meeting, Roy Fedden, a design engineer at Bristol Aircraft Company and Leslie Frise, the designer of the "Frise aileron", stated that the design of the Beaufort Bomber could be converted into a fighter and argued that it would make sense to concentrate on that rather than building more Beauforts. Due to the lack of long range, cannon armed fighters, and after some persuasion, the Air Ministry agreed and the Beaufighter was born.

First flown in July 1939 it retained the Beaufort's wings, undercarriage and tail but had a smaller fuselage and more powerful Hercules engines. After disappointing initial kill rates the later Beaufighters had airborne interception radar fitted and were armed with four cannon and six Browning machine guns, significantly improving results. Four bombs were added to its arsenal in 1941.

During World War II, the Beaufighter played a significant role in the Battle of Britain, protecting the skies over the south of England. Flying at night, all-black painted Beaufighters acted as "Night Interceptors" in the hands of skilled pilots such as Grp Captain John 'Cats-Eyes' Cunningham who was credited with the highest number of 'Night Kills'

Nicknamed "Cats' Eyes," a sobriquet that Cunningham never liked, his exceptional skill on the nocturnal battlefield was put down to eating carrots to improve his night vision.

This rather romantic explanation for his success was promoted by the government in an attempt to hide the fact that British scientists had secretly developed a sophisticated and formidable airborne radar system. The new system allowed pilots to home in on Luftwaffe bomber formations, often with devastating consequences.

Concorde

When I left school in 1963 my friend, Geoffrey Capstick, atended Filton Technical College and started work for BAC in the offices. When I used to pick him up to go out for the night, playing darts or going to see the latest film, he would often tell me about a project they were working on to produce a supersonic passenger aircraft, He even had a very futuristic looking poster of it on his wall. Despite our mutual friend Alan and I both being interested in anything aviation related, we took it all with a pinch of salt, thinking that supersonic airliners were probably as far into the future as landing on the moon. No vision you see, that was my trouble.

The 1950s was the decade of supersonic flight. The sound barrier had been broken and the race was on to build a supersonic airliner. At BAC in Bristol, Archibald E Russell led a team that designed the Bristol Type 198 aircraft. Powered by six Rolls-Royce Olympus engines the team was confident the aircraft would reach at least Mach 2.2 but it was never built. The government thought it too expensive and suggested BAC should turn their efforts towards something smaller. The next project Russell's team took on was the four engine Type 223 which turned out to be similar in design to an aircraft being developed by Sud Aviation in France, the Super Caravelle. On the 29th November 1962 the British and French governments agreed to finance a joint project to develop a supersonic civil airliner.

In 1960, the British Aircraft Corporation took over the aircraft interests of the Bristol Aeroplane Company. In the early 1960s a new Filton bypass was constructed, roughly parallel to the old one, and this later became part of the M5 motorway. The 1960s and 1970s saw the development and production of Concorde at Filton. The first flight of the Concorde 002 prototype took place on 9 April 1969 at Filton Aerodrome. All other British-built Concordes also used the main Filton runway for their first flights. Because of jet blast, gates and traffic lights were installed to close off the A38 road when Concorde took off.

International Balloon Festival at Ashton Court Estate

When I first started gliding at Nympsfied there was a man who would sometimes enlist the help of members to launch a hot-air balloon, long before it became a popular sport. It was only sometime later that I realised it was Don Cameron, later to become one of the world's most famous balloon manufacturers.

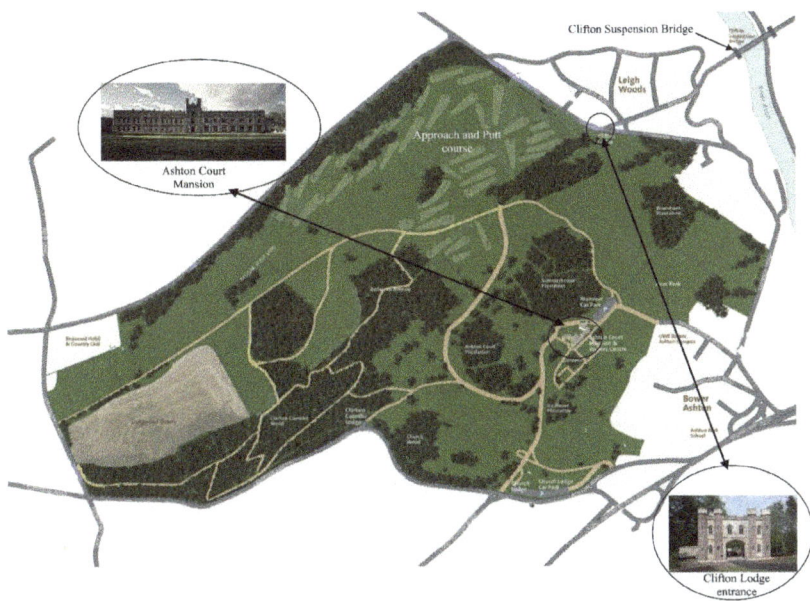

Ashton Court Estate

Ashton Court has been the site of a manor house since the 11th century, and has been developed by a series of owners since then. From the 16th to 20th centuries, it was owned by the Smyth family with each generation changing the house.

It was used as a military hospital in the First World War. In 1936 it was used as the venue for the Royal show and, during the Second World War as an army transit camp. In 1946 the last of the Smyth family died and the house fell into disrepair before its purchase in 1959 by Bristol City Council.

The estate developed from the original deer park and it is believed that a fortified manor stood on the site, given to Geoffrey de Montblloonray, Bishop of Coutnances by William the Conqueror and is listed in the Domesday Book.

The property passed through successive owners and at the end of the 14th century it was considerably expanded when

Thomas De Lions, a nobleman originally from France, obtained a permit to enclose a park for his manor.

The house was owned by the Choke family for some time, and In 1506 it was sold to Sir Giles Daubeney, a knight and a Chamberlain of Henry VIII. The estate then passed into the hands of Sir Thomas Arundel in1541 and four years later it was sold to John Smyth. Smyth also bought land that, before the dissolution of the monasteries, had been owned by Bath Abby.

The estate was owned by the Smyth family for 400 years, and was altered extensively in 1635 when Thomas Smyth added a new southern front which was in the style of Indigo Jones. Further major additions were made to the building in the 18th century by Sir John Hugh Smyth and by Sir Greville Smyth in 1872, shortly before he married Emily, the widow of George Oldham Edwards. Sir Greville Smyth died in 1901 and Lady Emily Smyth died in 1914.

The last residents of the house were Gilbert and Esme Smyth. They lived there for the next thirty years. Gilbert died in 1940 and Esme in 1946 and the house was left to their daughter Esme Francis Cavendish. She and her husband tried to sell the house immediately in 1946 to help pay the death duties, however it wasn't until 1959, during which time the house was unoccupied and had started to decay that they managed to sell it to Bristol City Council, who still own it.

For most of the 20th century Ashton Court has been the venue for a number of festivals and exhibitions including the North Somerset Show, which is now held elsewhere.

Between 1974 and 2007 the Ashton Court Festival was held in the grounds of the estate. The festival was a weekend event which featured a variety of local bands and national headliners, but unlike most successful music festivals it lacked overnight camping facilities.

Bristol Mass Assent

Unfortunately, although growing in popularity, changes to government legislation, resulted compulsory fees being introduced and security fencing being installed, this together with problems due to flooding and foot and mouth, eventually led to the organisers declaring bankruptcy in 2007.

The estate and grounds are now best known for the internationally famous Bristol International Balloon Festival, with its mass assents and night glow highlights.

Bristol Night Glow

Bristol Blue Glass

Bristol Blue Glass

During the late 18th century Richard Champion, a Bristol merchant and potter, making Bristol porcelain, was working with a chemist, William Cookworthy, began a search for good quality cobalt oxide to give the blue glaze decoration on white porcelain and obtained exclusive import rights to all the cobalt oxide from the Royal Saxon Cobalt Works in Saxony.

It is uncertain when Bristol blue glass was first made but the quality and beauty of the glass swiftly gained popularity, with seventeen glass houses being set up in the city.

Lazarus and Isaac Jacobs were the most famous makers of Bristol blue glass in the 1780s. Lazarus Jacobs was a Jewish immigrant to Bristol from Frankfurt am Main, Germany. In 1774, at the age of seventeen, Isaac joined his father's glass cutting firm at 108 Temple Street, Bristol, and launched Bristol Blue glass as a national brand, using the cobalt oxide Cookworthy imported. Isaac was responsible for the great growth of the company, and the expansion of its goods.[4] Their company held a royal warrant and made glass for the aristocrats of Europe.[5] Bristol's glass makers were invited to demonstrate their skills at the Great Exhibition of 1851, opened by Queen Victoria and Prince Albert. At this period cranberry glass was made for the first time by adding 24 carat gold to lead crystal, giving the glass its ruby red tones. Production ceased in about 1923.

Bristol-based glass makers James Adlington and Peter Sinclair held their Hot Glass exhibition in 1988 at Hand Made Glass, Bristol. This exhibition led to a revival of Bristol's hand blown glass industry and the creation of a Company that has spawned the careers of many other studio Glassmakers in the South west. Today, Bristol Blue Glass is produced by The Original Bristol Blue Glass Ltd in Brislington, established in 1988.

In the 1990s, John Harvey & Sons of Bristol began to sell Bristol Cream sherry in bottles made from Bristol blue.

Chapter 13

Oh! I Almost Forgot

The memory works in mysterious ways, well mine does anyway.

My father's van BBX 491 was something like the one depicted here

For instance, I have never been able to remember any of my car registration numbers, not one. However, when we first moved to St Michael's Hill from Cotham Hill, I can remember that my father owned a little green van, probably a Bedford 5 Cwt, but for some extrodinary reason I remember that it's registration number was BBX 491!

I've no idea why I remember that, so here are some more of my memories that I either wasn't sure where to include, or has only just come to mind reading through what I've already written. I suppose if I'd realised things were changing so much thoughout the fifties and sixties I might have taken more notice at the time. I might even have made more use of the box-brownie or later the Ilford camera and flash I had, or my brother's Kodak 127, but unfortunately I didn't.

The two cameras I remember in the fifties

What I do remember is how much more complicated it was to load a camera back then.

loading film into a camera

First you had to open the back of the camera and feed the end of the roll of film through the slot in the take up spool, locate the new film roll in the space for the films spool and secure in place, take up any slack in the film and close the back of the camera, ensuring that the lugs on the carriage spool engage in the holes on the edge of the roll.

There would be a lever on the top of the camera to wind the film on to the the next available area of unexposed film, so this would be used to advance the film to the first position.

Then after the first picture was taken, you had to the wind the film on again before taking the next. When all the roll was used, it had to be rolled completely onto the one spool, before the back of the camera was opened in a darkened room, and the roll of film placed in its black plastic container. This would then be sent off to the developer. You would then have to wait anxiously for the pictures to come back from the developers before you could see how disappointing your holiday snaps were. Normally 20% would go in the family album, 20 % in the loft or odd drawer and 60% in the rubbish bin. Oh yes, and if you wanted to use flash there was normally a separate flashgun that could be fitted to the camera, and the flash bulb itself would have to be replaced each time.

If you wanted to buy a camera back then, you had the option of paying for it with green shield stamps.

This was a British sales promotion scheme that rewarded shoppers with stamps that could be used to buy gifts from a catalogue.

A Green Shield Stamp

The promotion was introduced in 1958 because of the success a similar scheme was having in America.

For a few years, the scheme was so widely adopted that most food stores offered stamps. It began to suffer when Tesco stopped giving stamps and adopted a price-cutting policy that became standard nationwide. To retain business, Green Shield allowed customers to buy gifts from the catalogue with a mix of stamps and cash, but soon the catalogue became cash-only, and the operation was re-branded as Argos.

You didn't need to collect stamp to purchase items from catalogues however.

Advert from a mail order catalouge

My mother's friend who we all knew as Mrs. Smith, would visit every Saturday morning with fresh baked cobs, and a couple of catalogues. It soon became almost a family tradition. She was an agent for at least two catalogues and would earn commission on any orders placed.

She made quality curtains in a shop further down Chandos Road, and would sell any remaining material to my farther for upholstery. I can remember buying some tools and a very trendy Safari Jacket from one of her catalogues.

I did notice a couple of changes in fashion of course, once I was old enough to appreciate such things as girls and their hemlines. I was delighted to see skirts getting shorter in the sixties! I had been too young to realise that after the war, skirts had actually become longer, probably as a reaction to the fact that material had been in short supply during rationing. Remember boys wore short trousers until senior school as part of the war effort.

I can also remember that my father had some shirts with separate collars, that had to be attached with collar studs! How weird was that? It was a practical thing I suppose, instead of having a clean shirt every day, you could just have a clean collar. Whereas a lady or gentleman would have a leather box for their hat when travelling, a gentleman would always have a box for his collar and studs,

Two other items of men's attire that went out of fashion were hats and ties. Whereas in the thirties and forties you would seldom see a man without a hat of one sort or another, usually a trilby or a flat cap, it was much more of a rarity in my time, unless it was raining. As for wearing a tie, even in the fifties, it may have been acceptable to go without one on the beach or at home, but never at work or out and about in public. You even put on your Sunday best to go to the cinema.

Speaking of the cinema, if you wanted an ice-cream or fruit drink or popcorn, an usherette would come in and stand with a tray of such things to buy during the intermission, and I can remember that we always tried to leave the auditorium before the film credits had finished, otherwise we would have to stand for the National Anthem.

Talking about changes to what was acceptable to do in public back then, compared to now, eating in the street was frowned on, at least by my mother. It was only ever done late at night, on the way home from the cinema, and it had to be fish and chips from a newspaper.

When we moved into Chandos Road there was a barber's shop just a dozen doors away, so I would walk up there after school if I needed a haircut. When I had left school and the barber became more chatty, he started asking me about work and football. Why he asumed I was a football fan I don't know. Every time I sat in his chair and he asked me how I would like my hair cut, I was tempted to reply, "In silence," but always said "Just a trim and a tapered back not square." When he began asking me if I needed anything for the weekend, I wasn't sure what he meant, and just thought maybe he was asking if I wanted some aftershave or Brylcream. It was some time later that a friend informed me that a barber's shop always sold condoms, and most men would buy them there rather than a Chemist shop.

It was also a time when I remember talk about smokeless fuel and smog, and I do remember seeing a very dense fog that people referred to as a pea-souper.

The Great Smog of London, or Great Smog of 1952, was a severe air pollution event that affected London, in December 1952. A period of unusually cold weather, combined with an anticyclone and windless conditions, collected airborne pollutants (mostly arising from the use of coal) to form a thick layer of smog over the city. It lasted from Friday 5th December to Tuesday 9th December 1952.

It caused major disruption by reducing visibility and even penetrating indoor areas, far more severely than previous smog events, called "pea-soupers". Government medical reports in the weeks following the event estimated that up to 4,000 people had died as a direct result of the smog and 100,000 more were made ill by the smog's effects on the human respiratory tract. More recent research suggests that the total number of fatalities may have been considerably greater, with estimates of between 10,000 and 12,000 deaths.

The Clean Air Act 1956 was an Act of the Parliament of the United Kingdom enacted principally in response to London's Great Smog of 1952. It was sponsored by the Ministry of Housing and Local Government in England and the Department of Health for Scotland, and was in effect until 1993.

It introduced several measures to reduce air pollution. Primary among them was mandated movement toward smokeless fuels, especially in high-population "smoke control areas" to reduce smoke pollution and sulphur dioxide from household fires. The Act also included measures that reduced the emission of gases, grit, and dust from chimneys and smoke-stacks.

I've spoken to quite a few people of my generation about the kind of meals the family would have eaten back then, and a surprisingly large number said that they always knew what was for dinner, because they had set meals for each day of the week, and this was certainly the case in our house. I can always remember that we had roast beef on Sundays for lunch, with bread and dripping for supper. Mondays would usually be cold beef left over from Sunday with fried egg and bubble and squeak. Tuesdays was a fry-up, Wednesdays was breast of lamb with boiled potatoes, Thursday sausage and mash, Friday was fish, and Saturday, could be either minced beef and mash, curry which was basically minced beef flavoured with curry powder and served with boiled rice, or boiled ham with mashed potatoes and baked beans. At some time during the summer, one of the aforementioned meals would be replaced with a salad. Desserts alternated between spotted dick, jam roly-poly rice pudding or milk macaroni.

Very few working-class families would go out to a restaurant for a meal, unless they were on holiday or it was a special occasion, and apart from spaghetti, any foreign cuisine was almost unknown. The only Chinese restaurant that I can remember was one on Whiteladies Road.

In the sixties and early seventies dinner parties become popular, and hosts would serve new fashionable 'foreign' dishes like Spaghetti Bolognese, often accompanied by wines such as Blue Nun, Chianti and Mateus Rose.

Also at this time, the chains of restaurants "Berni Inns" began to appear in Bristol. The Rummer, The Hole in the Wall, and the Llandoger Trow, were all serving the classic 1970s favourites of Melon or Prawn Cocktail, Mixed Grill or Steak, and Black Forest Gateau or Lemon Meringue Pie for dessert.

Television sets were black and white, and a lot of older people would only watch BBC even if they had access to the new ITV channel. BBC 1 launched a full colour service on 15th November 1969. At midnight, *An Evening with Petula* - Petula Clark in concert from the Royal Albert Hall, was the first transmission. The channel then closed down until 10am. Programmes showing in colour on the 15th included *Star Trek* and *Dixon of Dock Green*, *The Harry Secombe Show* and *Match of the Day*, plus the feature film *The Prisoner of Zenda*. Back then you could either purchase a television set or rent one if you preferred. When I was first married and living in Longfield Road, Eileen and I would sometimes walk Cleo, our dog after dark.
If we saw a light on in the room of a house and the curtains were open, Eileen would always announce before we got there, "I'll bet they've got a colour television, and they want the neighbours to know." She was nearly always right.

My brother was born in October 1941 and must have missed conscription by the skin of his teeth. I mention this because, the two conflicts I remember hearing about in the fifties were the Korean War and the Suez Crisis.
The Korean War began in 1950 and the fighting ended with an armistice in 1953. All I can remember is being taken, to see a film called "A Hill in Korea." It was released in 1956, and featured Michael Caine in his first credited film role. Caine had a small part because of his experience in the Korean War, where he had served as a soldier. He later said, "My function as a technical adviser was completely ignored during the making of the film." For that reason he added, "I never brought to their notice that Portugal did not in the least resemble Korea; if anything, Wales was more similar. I did not say anything

because I wanted to stay in Portugal; I could go to Wales at any old time. I had eight lines in that picture, and I screwed up six of them." According to Caine, "the company held on to the film for ages before releasing it. After a year of waiting for the perfect moment, with true movie genius they premiered the film on the night that we invaded Suez."

The Suez Canal was financed by the French and Egyptian governments and opened in 1869, after ten years of work, and was operated by an Egyptian-chartered company. The area surrounding the canal remained sovereign Egyptian territory. By 1955, petroleum accounted for half of the canal's traffic, and, in turn, two thirds of Europe's oil passed through it.

After the Second World War, Britain's military strength was spread wide, including a garrison of some 80,000 men at Suez, making it one of the largest military installations in the world. The Suez base was considered an important part of Britain's strategic position in the Middle East; however, it became a source of growing tension between Egypt and Britain.

Egypt's post-war domestic politics were experiencing a radical change, prompted in no small part by economic instability, inflation, and unemployment. Unrest began to manifest itself in the growth of radical political groups, and an increasingly hostile attitude towards Britain and its presence in the country. Adding to this anti-British feeling was the role Britain had played in the creation of Israel after the war.

In October 1951, the Egyptian government unilaterally revoked the treaty of 1936 that granted Britain a lease on the Suez base for 20 more years. Britain refused to withdraw from Suez, relying upon its treaty rights, as well as the presence of the Suez garrison. The price of such a course of action was a steady escalation in violent hostility towards Britain and British troops in Egypt, which the Egyptian authorities did little to curb.

In 1952 Gamal Abdul Nasser overthrew King Farouk and nationalised the Suez Canal Company, which prior to that was owned primarily by British and French shareholders, and on 29th October, Israel invaded the Egyptian Sinai.

Britain and France issued a joint ultimatum to cease fire, which was ignored, so on 5th November, Britain and France landed para troops along the Suez Canal, but before the Egyptian forces were defeated, they had blocked the canal to all shipping by sinking 40 ships in the canal. It later became clear that Israel, France and Britain had conspired to plan the invasion. The three allies had attained a number of their military objectives, but the canal was useless.

Heavy political pressure from the United States and the USSR led to a withdrawal. U.S. president Dwight D. Eisenhower had strongly warned Britain not to invade; he threatened serious damage to the British financial system by selling the U.S. government's pound sterling bonds. (Obviously an example of the Special relationship.)

The Suez Canal was closed from October 1956 until March 1957. Israel fulfilled some of its objectives, such as attaining freedom of navigation through the Straits of Tiran, which Egypt had blocked to Israeli shipping since 1948–1950.

As a result of the conflict, the United Nations created the UNEF Peacekeepers to police the Egyptian–Israeli border, and prime minister Anthony Eden resigned. Canadian external affairs minister Lester Pearson won the Nobel Peace Prize, and the USSR may have been emboldened to invade Hungary.

Earlier in the book I mentioned the Eileen and I became friendly with Doug and Maureen and started going out for meals regularly with them in a group that included, Doug's brother Bob and his wife Joyce plus the couple who ran the fish and chip shop opposite the workshop, John and Sheila. John had a reputation as somebody with lots of contacts who could get anything you wanted. We wanted a larger compressor for the spray booth and Doug wondered if it was something John could get.

"Leave it with me" he said. and a week later a delivery van turned up with a new compressor.

The one we were replacing was tiny compared. This monster that arrived was the size of a domestic oil tank, and could run five spay guns. It was also German and there was no instructions, other that in German.

The air tank had several threaded ports that had nylon buns screwed in to protect the threads. We were careful to replace all the nylon bungs with the brass ones supplied or an outlet for a gun. The one exception being the pressure gauge.

When we were sure all was well, we turned it on and anxiously watch as the pressure built up.

What we hadn't spotted because the tank was so large and heavy to lift was a nylon bung underneath the tank. This was, we realised later, so a drain tap could be inserted for any condensation build up inside the tank.

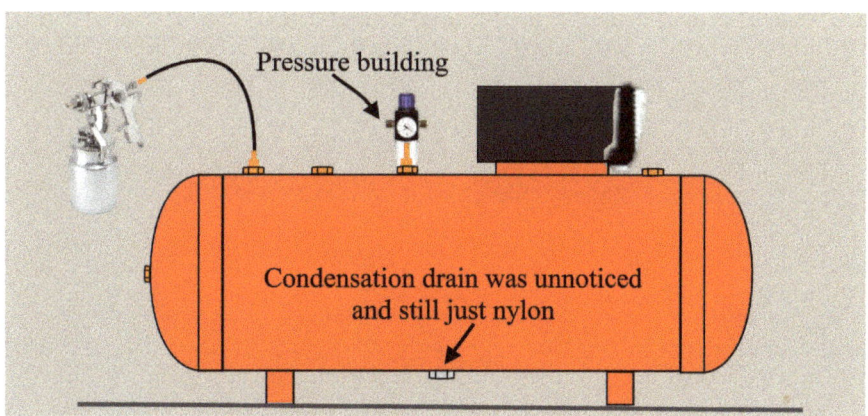

Pressure built up until the nylon bung gave out

It is difficult to convey the panic amongst those present when the pressure eventually shot the treaded bung out so close to a dusty concrete floor. It caused a horrendous bang accompanied by billowing dust and debris. We all believed that the entire thing had blown up!

Well, there we are. No doubt as soon this book is published, I will remember something else of interest, and I shall regret not including it. Or I will read the book and think to myself, why on earth did I include that, it's not that interesting or relevant.

To sum up, Eileen and I have just celebrated our golden wedding anniversary and we have two wonderful daughters and three lovely granddaughters and have generally been very lucky. So for family, and anyone who may be interested, I have attempted to put together a family tree overleaf.

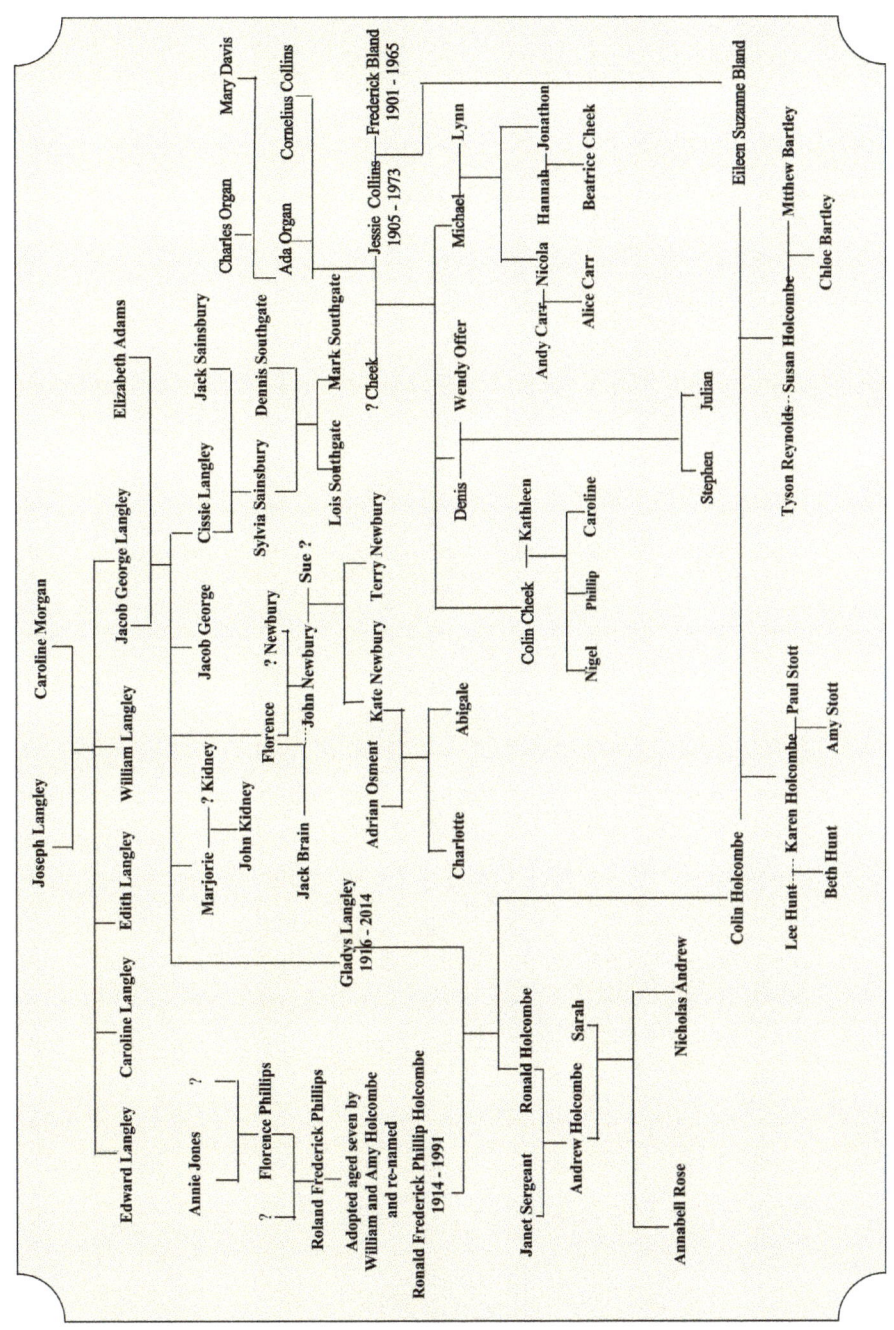

Family Tree

www.ingramcontent.com/pod-product-compliance
Lightning Source LLC
Chambersburg PA
CBHW051542010526
44118CB00022B/2556